THE Traveling VEGAN COOKBOOK

Exciting Plant-Based Meals from the Mediterranean, East Asia, the Middle East *and more*

KIRSTEN KAMINSKI

Founder of The Tasty K and author
of *Vegan Holiday Cooking*

PAGE STREET
PUBLISHING CO.

First published in 2021 by

Page Street Publishing Co.

27 Congress Street, Suite 105

Salem, MA 01970

www.pagestreetpublishing.com

Distributed by Macmillan, sales in Canada by The Canadian Manda Group.

25   24   23   22   21   1   2   3   4   5

ISBN-13: 978-1-64567-269-2

ISBN-10: 1-64567-269-7

Library of Congress Control Number: 2020945240

Cover and book design by Kylie Alexander for Page Street Publishing Co.

Photography by Kirsten Kaminski

Printed and bound in the United States

table of contents

Introduction

Hi there, I'm Kirsten. Some of you may know me from my Facebook page and Instagram account, The Tasty K, which has grown into one of the biggest vegan and travel-related video blogs sharing colorful plant-based recipes from all around the world.

If you're completely new to the vegan lifestyle, welcome! I published my first book, *Vegan Holiday Cooking*, in 2019, and I'm very excited to be back with even more delicious vegan recipes inspired by my travels during the past 10 years.

Traveling and experiencing different cultures and people has always fascinated me. While I was born and raised in a small city in Germany, my desire to leave my home country and explore the world started early. At 16 years old I decided to pack my bags and leave everything familiar behind to move to Mexico alone, which turned out to be one of the best decisions in my life. Once I caught the travel bug, I quickly finished high school back in Germany and continued my journey around the globe. Over the past 10 years I've lived in nine countries, including Spain, the Netherlands, Turkey, France, Israel, Thailand and the Greek part of Cyprus. My travels have also led me to Japan, Brazil, Jordan, all throughout Europe and the United States. Just last year I decided to move back to Germany and enjoy the buzzing vegan food scene in Berlin for a while.

For me, cooking and eating have always been very much connected to emotions, memories and experiences. As I turned vegan and became more passionate about cooking, my travels have, of course, inspired my creations. I would say that the places I've traveled, as well as memories of dishes I ate while growing up, are the biggest inspirations behind my recipes. Traveling and especially living abroad not only enriched me with many new experiences, but also led me to have a more open-minded approach to different cultures and their ways of cooking and eating.

Food is one of our simplest pleasures. No matter whether you are a foodie or just eat to live, it's likely that the memories of your last trip abroad are strongly connected to food. Food connects people. Every country and culture has its own unique ingredients, herbs and spices, and traditional foods that bring people together.

This book combines my two favorite things: food and travel. My travel experiences have greatly inspired me to experiment with new flavors and ingredients and ultimately led to the creation of each and every one of the wonderful dishes in this book. It's a compilation of my most cherished food memories and the many countries and cultures I have been lucky to taste. I invite you to refine your taste buds, open your senses and delve into extraordinary worlds of exciting flavors, colors and spices.

I encourage you to enter the kitchen with an open mind. Be creative, try new flavors and ingredients, and you'll likely create unforgettable culinary memories. I hope this book will ignite your curiosity to wander outside of your comfort zone—and fill lots of hungry bellies!

With love,

Kirsten Kaminski

Traveling as a Vegan

For me, a big part of traveling is experiencing the country's cuisine in an authentic way, which is why I'd rather not eat another vegan burger but instead stick to local flavors and tastes. But when you are traveling the world as a vegan, it will undoubtedly be harder than it is in your hometown to find suitable food choices.

You will quickly become aware of the many differences in food culture and eating habits around the world—and also the privilege of being able to choose what you want to eat and what you do not. Depending on where you go, people might eat a mostly vegetarian or even vegan diet simply because they cannot afford meat or fish, which are often way more expensive than local plant-based foods. In other places, the majority of dishes might be plant-based by default, due to people's beliefs and cultural values. Sometimes it might seem as if everyone is eating an animal-based diet and you will not be able to find vegan options at all. But you will!

Practical Tips and Tricks

Some countries and cuisines are naturally more vegan-friendly than others. But with a few tips and tricks, you can get along and find delicious vegan food everywhere.

Knowledge is power.

When traveling to a new country, the first thing I do is try to learn as much as possible about the culture and local cuisine. What kind of staple foods, such as grains and legumes, do people eat? What fruits and vegetables are native to the region and in season when I will be there? What herbs and spices are used? Staples and fresh produce will vary by region, and so will the dishes prepared with them.

In many places, usually where the diet includes a higher percentage of fresh ingredients, many traditional plates will be vegan already (such as hummus, falafel, dolmades, fava dip, pizza marinara and dhal). Other dishes can easily be "veganized" by simply removing one or two ingredients (pad Thai without the fish sauce or sabich without the egg on top).

In some parts of the world, dietary choices are connected to strong cultural and religious beliefs that promote vegetarianism and veganism, so people will already be accustomed to and more knowledgeable about plant-based cooking. Did you know that traditional Japanese Buddhist cuisine (shojin ryori) is predominantly vegan? Or that followers of Jainism in India believe in nonviolence toward all living beings and hence eat a strictly vegan diet?

Depending on where you are in the world, the dietary choices may be affected by religion, traditions, or ethical concerns, and it can be very helpful to know about them in advance.

Get online.

It can be helpful to join local vegan Facebook groups as a resource before you start your journey. In addition, there are groups dedicated to vegan traveling where people share lots of photos and recommendations. Download apps like HappyCow to find all the local vegan and vegan-friendly places near your destination. Looking back, there were many times when I was pleasantly surprised by the hidden treasures I found this way.

At the same time, try to look out for hidden, not so obvious non-vegan ingredients that are used a lot in certain cuisines, such as bonito fish flakes in Japanese cuisine and lard in some Latin American dishes. Vegan blogs and travel guides are a valuable asset for this kind of information.

Break the language barrier.

If I don't speak the language of the country I want to visit, I make sure to learn how to say certain keywords, such as "vegan," "dairy," "meat," "fish" and "eggs," as well as how to ask for a dish without these ingredients. Knowing what to say can be crucial in certain situations, especially if you're traveling in more rural areas. Just in case your pronunciation isn't the best, also make sure to write down those words and phrases and keep them handy, so you can just pull them out and point.

Snacks!

If you're traveling by plane to a far-away destination, call the airline at least 72 hours before your flight to request vegan options. Even if the airline guarantees vegan food, my biggest recommendation is to always have a variety of tasty snacks ready to go. Once you've reached your destination, you can scour local markets for exotic dried fruits, spiced nuts or other delicacies, but en route it is important to bring snacks you know you can eat.

Be creative.

Whenever you eat out, try to be creative. If a dish isn't vegan, ask if you can replace some ingredients for others (for example, replace the meat with beans in a burrito). Most restaurants and vendors will happily try to accommodate your needs, especially if you're attempting to speak their language. If they don't have any vegan dishes at all, scan the menu for what they do serve that you can eat, and ask if they can throw something tasty together for you. Also, if you can't be sure whether a dish is 100 percent vegan or perhaps contains a bit of chicken broth or egg, don't fret over it. It's not about purity or being perfect, but about doing your best to minimize suffering.

Go shopping and ask the locals.

Research the local food markets in the area and go wild. They will be filled with tons of beautiful fresh and exotic produce, snacks and other randomly vegan goodies. If you find a health food store or café, ask if they know any good vegan-friendly spots. Sometimes there are smaller, hidden gems with the best food that only the locals know.

Get cooking!

See if you can take local cooking classes. In many cities, local vegans or popular vegan chefs and food bloggers will organize cooking classes for visitors. For example, in Bangkok you can find May Kaidee's phenomenal vegan Thai cooking workshop. It's not only a great way to meet people but also to experience a country's cuisine in a very authentic way.

Vegan-Friendly Countries

During my travels over the past 10 years, I have had mixed experiences when it comes to finding great vegan food. While some countries surprised me with a booming vegan scene as well as a vast array of traditional dishes that were vegan by default, other places were a bit more difficult to navigate food-wise. Below you'll find a short list of countries that really impressed me or are known to be vegan foodie heaven.

Israel

Did you know that Israel is the most vegan country per capita? A whopping 13 percent of Israelis identify as vegetarian, while 5.2 percent are vegan—numbers that are rapidly increasing. Tel Aviv has repeatedly been declared the vegan capital of the world with more than 400 restaurants that are considered vegan-friendly and new ones popping up every week or so ("vegan-friendly" means at least 25 percent of menu items are plant-based).

Due to the sun-kissed climate, high-quality produce is never hard to find. You can see it in the colorful creations, taste it in the flavors and smell it in the aromas of what's on your plate. Many of Israel's most popular traditional dishes, like hummus, falafel and baba ganoush, are already vegan. Hence plant-based cooking is not only thriving but highly demanded by the 1 million Israelis who don't eat meat—most of whom are living in Tel Aviv. Even big brands like Domino's and Ben & Jerry's have jumped on the vegan bandwagon, using Israel as a test market for their newest dairy-free products. Israel is also the world leader in lab-grown meat.

Why do so many Israelis choose a lifestyle without animal products? Israel is a young country with immigrants who come from all over the world, bringing their own cultures and cuisines. Some people argue that because of that, Israeli culture is still evolving and the people are less attached to traditional ways of eating. As a start-up nation open to innovation, Israelis are eager to try new things, including in the culinary world.

Thailand

Thailand has been one of my favorite countries to visit as a vegan. You will find fruit stands on every corner and fresh local markets are abundant. Traditionally, many Asian, specifically Thai, staples are vegan by default, so many dishes are either completely plant-based or easily customizable. Just be aware that many dishes are prepared with fish sauce or chicken broth, so just ask to leave them out. While in some countries there is no widely understood translation of the word "vegan," in Thailand this is not a problem. The concept of veganism, or jay (เจ), has been around for hundreds of years in Thailand and is connected with Buddhist practices.

Australia

Veganism has become hugely popular in Australia as more and more Aussies are turning to a plant-based diet. In 2018, Australia was the third fastest-growing market for vegan products. Sydney and Melbourne can regularly be found among the world's top 20 vegan cities.

Canada

More than 3 million Canadians are either vegan or vegetarian. Mostly young Canadians are driving the change in eating habits; the younger generation is three times more likely to be either vegetarian or vegan than older generations. Toronto has long been known in the vegan scene for hosting one of the largest vegetarian events in North America—Toronto Veg Food Fest—and the number of vegan restaurants in the city continues to grow by the week.

Greece

This may not seem obvious, but the Mediterranean Greek diet is actually heavily plant-based. Thanks to the Greek Orthodox fasting traditions, several times a year (more than 180 days) you'll commonly find dishes that do not include animal products to adhere to the rules of the fast. Such foods are called nistisima (νηστίσιμα, a helpful word to learn), and for many dishes you'll find a nistisimo version (just specify without seafood or honey, as those can be exceptions).

United States

A whopping 4 to 5 percent of Americans are now vegan—up 600 percent in three years. Veganism has become extremely popular in certain areas of the United States. You'll regularly find several American cities in the world's top 20 vegan metropolises. With its incredibly diverse variety of cuisines, New York's vegan scene continues to flourish. There are 111 vegan restaurants within a five-mile radius of the city. Similarly, vegan mecca Los Angeles has 49 fully vegan and another 190 vegetarian and vegan-friendly restaurants in a five-square-mile area.

THE MEDITERRANEAN

Filled with fresh vegetables and herbs, tasty legumes, rich oils and whole grains, the cuisine of the Mediterranean is abundantly rich in plants. While most Southern European countries, like Greece, Italy, France and Portugal, also eat a lot of animal products, it is easy to substitute them and you can find many dishes that are traditionally vegan.

Whether you're looking for that deliciously sweet custard tart from Lisbon (page 47), your favorite French crêpes (page 43), the best vegan pizza with stretchy mozzarella (page 22) or an overflowing Greek mezze platter (page 25), I've got you covered.

VEGAN PIZZA

A staple in any Italian diet, I had to include pizza! I still have the flavors of my first real Italian pizza in Milano lingering in my memory from many years ago. Let's all agree here that although there are some traditional vegan Italian variations, pizza without cheese is pretty boring. Don't worry though, this vegan version is perfectly stretchy and even melts. This recipe makes two individual pizzas, so everyone can top theirs just the way they like. Invite your friends, add your favorite toppings and throw a vegan pizza party!

Serves 2

To make the dough, combine 1 cup (240 ml) of warm water with the sugar and yeast in a small bowl and set aside for 10 minutes. Place the flour and salt in a medium bowl and combine. Add the yeast mixture and knead by gently but firmly pushing the dough down and away from you with the heels of your hands for 2 to 3 minutes, adding flour as needed. If you have an appliance that kneads dough, you can let it do the work for you. The dough should not be too dry nor too sticky. Lightly grease a medium bowl, place the dough in it, cover with a towel and let it rise in a warm place for 1½ to 2 hours, until it has doubled in size.

In the meantime, prepare the cheeses. For the almond cheese, simply place all the ingredients, plus ½ to ¾ cup (120 to 180 ml) of water (depending on the consistency you prefer), in a food processor and blend until smooth, 1 to 2 minutes. Transfer the cheese to a container, cover and let chill in the fridge.

For the mozzarella, combine all the ingredients, plus 1½ cups (360 ml) of water, in a high-speed blender and blend for 1 to 2 minutes, until it's completely smooth. Pour the mixture into a medium saucepan and place over medium heat. Cook for 60 to 90 seconds, stirring continuously, as the mozzarella firms up and gets stretchy. Take the pan off the heat, pour the cheese into a glass jar, cover and place it in the fridge to chill.

Preheat the oven to 425°F (220°C). Line a baking tray with parchment paper.

(continued)

Dough

1 tsp sugar

1 tsp active dry yeast

2 cups (250 g) all-purpose flour

½ tsp salt

Almond Cheese

1½ cups (225 g) blanched almonds, soaked in water overnight

2 tbsp (10 g) nutritional yeast

3 tbsp (45 ml) lemon juice

1 tbsp (15 ml) apple cider vinegar

3 tbsp (45 ml) extra-virgin olive oil

1 clove garlic, peeled

1 tsp salt

½ tsp garlic powder

Vegan Mozzarella

¼ cup (35 g) raw cashews, soaked in water overnight

2 tbsp (30 ml) refined melted coconut oil (see Note)

2 tbsp (10 g) nutritional yeast

1 tsp lemon juice

1 tsp apple cider vinegar

1 tsp agar powder

2½ tbsp (25 g) tapioca starch

½ tsp salt

Pinch of ground nutmeg

VEGAN PIZZA (CONTINUED)

Divide the dough in half. You can either bake both pizzas at the same time on one baking tray (and shape them accordingly) or using two small round pans, or bake them one after another. Use a rolling pin to roll out the first piece of dough on a floured surface, until you have a thin crust. Repeat with the other piece of dough. Transfer the flattened dough to the baking tray and top with as much marinara sauce as you like. Add some other toppings and a few tablespoons of each of the cheeses. Bake for 10 to 15 minutes, until the crust is golden brown and the mozzarella has melted. Cut and enjoy immediately.

Note: Refined or deodorized coconut oil means it has been processed for longer, resulting in a milder taste that is less coconutty.

Toppings

12 oz (340 g) marinara sauce

2 handfuls arugula (optional)

½ medium onion, sliced (optional)

1 tsp dried oregano (optional)

5 to 6 cremini mushrooms, sliced (optional)

Fresh basil

GREEK MEZZE

This vegan version of a Greek mezze platter has got me drooling and dwelling in memories of warm summer nights in small Greek taverns. There is nothing more fun than preparing and sharing a big and colorful table of beautiful fresh vegetable dishes. This platter has everything you might want: the perfect balance of fresh salads, creamy dips, tangy cheeses, flavorful spreads and, of course, the famous dolmades (stuffed grape leaves).

Serves 4

FAVA DIP

Place 2 tablespoons (30 ml) of oil in a saucepan over medium-high heat. Add the onion and sauté for 1 minute, then add the garlic and sauté for 15 seconds. Add the split peas and whisk together. Pour in 1½ to 2 cups (360 to 480 ml) of water (start with less and add more as needed), turn the heat down to medium, cover the pan and simmer for 15 to 20 minutes. Check from time to time and skim off any white foam that builds up on top.

When the peas are cooked and mushy, take them off the heat and set aside to cool. Transfer them to a food processor. Add the remaining 1 tablespoon (15 ml) of olive oil, lemon juice, salt and pepper, and blend. Don't worry if it seems a bit liquid; it will firm up as it cools. Place in a serving bowl and add the toppings.

3 tbsp (45 ml) extra-virgin olive oil, divided

1 medium red onion, diced

3 cloves garlic, sliced

1 cup (200 g) dry yellow split peas, rinsed and drained

2 tbsp (30 ml) lemon juice

½ tsp salt

¼ tsp black pepper

Toppings

1 tbsp (15 ml) lemon juice

1 tbsp (15 ml) extra-virgin olive oil

Dash of sweet paprika

TZATZIKI

To drain the cucumber, place it in a kitchen towel or cheesecloth, collect the ends and squeeze out as much liquid as possible. You should end up with about ¼ cup (30 g) of shredded cucumber after draining. Then simply mix all the ingredients in a medium bowl and whisk together. Add salt and pepper to taste.

1 cup (120 g) shredded cucumber

1 cup (250 g) unsweetened soy yogurt

1 to 2 cloves garlic, minced

1½ to 2 tbsp (22 to 30 ml) lemon juice

2 tbsp (7 g) chopped fresh dill

Salt

Pepper

(continued)

TOFU FETA

Drain and rinse your tofu block and place it between a number of folded paper towels. Place something heavy on top (like books or a cast-iron skillet) and let it sit for at least 1 hour. Then unwrap and dice the tofu.

Prepare the marinade by whisking together all the remaining ingredients, plus ½ cup (120 ml) of water, in a small bowl. Place the tofu cubes in an airtight jar, add the marinade, close the jar and gently shake for a few seconds to make sure the tofu is well coated. Refrigerate for at least 3 to 4 hours; it's even better overnight.

1 (7-oz (200-g)) block firm tofu

1 tsp white miso paste

2 tbsp (30 ml) extra-virgin olive oil

3 tbsp (45 ml) apple cider vinegar

¼ cup (60 ml) lemon juice

1 tbsp (5 g) nutritional yeast

1 tsp onion powder

1 tsp garlic powder

1 tbsp (5 g) dried oregano

½ to 1 tsp salt

KALAMATA TAPENADE

Add all the ingredients to a food processor and process for 30 to 60 seconds. Transfer to a jar and refrigerate until you are ready to use it.

3.5 oz (100 g) Kalamata olives, pitted

1 clove garlic

1 tbsp (9 g) capers, rinsed

1 tsp coarsely chopped fresh parsley

2 tbsp (30 ml) extra-virgin olive oil

Salt

Pepper

(continued)

LENTIL SALAD

In a small bowl, whisk all the dressing ingredients together until they are thoroughly blended. Set aside.

In a medium saucepan over high heat, bring 3 cups (720 ml) of water to a boil and add the lentils. Lower the heat to a gentle simmer, cover and cook for 20 to 25 minutes, until tender but not mushy. Drain the lentils and set aside to cool.

In a medium bowl, combine the olives, tomatoes, spinach, red onion, spring onion, sun-dried tomatoes, feta and almonds, and mix. When the lentils are cool, add them to the bowl. Pour over the dressing and toss until blended. Serve with extra Tofu Feta on top.

Dressing

¼ cup (60 ml) extra-virgin olive oil

1 tbsp (15 ml) red wine vinegar

1 tbsp (15 ml) lemon juice

1 tbsp (16 g) tahini

Salt

Pepper

1 cup (190 g) dry green lentils, soaked in water for 30 to 60 minutes, then drained and rinsed

4 tbsp (45 g) sliced Kalamata olives

6 cherry tomatoes, quartered

1 cup (30 g) baby spinach, roughly chopped

1 small red onion, diced

1 tbsp (4 g) minced spring onion

3 tbsp (12 g) sun-dried tomatoes packed in oil, rinsed and diced

⅓ cup (85 g) Tofu Feta (page 27), plus more for topping

2 tbsp (16 g) slivered almonds

DOLMADES

Fill a large pot with salted water and bring it to a boil over high heat. Trim the leaves by cutting off any hard veins and stems. Place the leaves in the boiling water and let them soften for 3 to 5 minutes, until they are pliable. Drain and carefully rinse with cold water, then pat them dry and set aside.

Heat up 3 tablespoons (45 ml) of the olive oil in a large skillet over medium-high heat. Add the onion and sauté for 1 minute, then add the garlic and sauté for another 30 to 40 seconds. Add the rice, tomato, dill, mint, parsley and broth and cook for 5 to 7 minutes. Remove from the heat, season with salt and pepper, and stir in the pine nuts. Set the mixture aside to cool down a little bit.

Line the bottom of a large pot or skillet with some of the grape leaves (the ones that have holes or cracks), with the shiny side down.

To assemble the dolmades, lay out a grape leaf, shiny side down, on a cutting board. Place about 2 tablespoons (30 g) of the rice filling at the base end of the leaf, close to where the stem was. Fold the stem end up over the filling, then fold the edges of the leaf inward and continue rolling it like a burrito. Make sure not to roll too tightly, as the rice will expand while cooking. Squeeze the roll gently to seal and repeat with the remaining leaves and rice mixture.

Place the stuffed leaves in the bottom of the leaf-lined pot. Pack them tightly together to prevent opening and stack layer over layer. Pour the remaining 5 tablespoons (75 ml) of olive oil and the lemon juice over the stuffed leaves and add water until the leaves are just covered. Place a plate on top of the leaves to prevent them from moving while cooking. Place the pot over medium heat, cover, and let it simmer (not boil) for 30 to 40 minutes, until the rice is cooked and the leaves are tender.

25 to 30 dried grape leaves

½ cup (120 ml) extra-virgin olive oil, divided

1 medium white onion, diced small

2 cloves garlic, minced

¾ cup (145 g) short-grain white rice, rinsed and drained

1 small tomato, finely chopped

3 tbsp (10 g) minced fresh dill

2 tbsp (11 g) minced fresh mint

1 tbsp (4 g) minced fresh parsley

¾ cup (180 ml) vegetable broth

Salt

Pepper

4 tbsp (34 g) pine nuts, toasted

2 tbsp (30 ml) lemon juice

(continued)

BAKED GIANT BEANS

Place the giant beans in a large bowl with a dash of baking soda and generously cover with water. Soak for 12 hours. Drain the water into a pot and rinse the beans. Place the pot over high heat and bring to a boil. Skim off any foam that is building up at the top. Scoop the rinsed beans into the pot in batches, then lower the heat to medium and simmer for 1 hour, until the beans soften. Drain and set aside.

Preheat the oven to 350°F (175°C).

Add the oil to a large pan and place over high heat. Add the onion and sauté for 3 to 4 minutes, then add the garlic and sauté another minute. Add the carrot and celery and cook for 5 minutes. Add the tomato paste, brown sugar and white wine and cook for 2 minutes. Add the diced tomatoes, 1 cup (240 ml) of water, the bay leaves, salt and pepper, cook for another 5 minutes, then remove the pot from the heat.

Transfer the sauce and the beans to a large ovenproof bean pot. Mix well, then close the lid and bake for 1 hour and 10 minutes. When the beans are nice and soft, they're done.

18 oz (510 g) dry gigantes (Greek giant beans), rinsed and drained

Dash of baking soda

3 tbsp (45 ml) extra-virgin olive oil

1 large yellow onion, diced small

3 cloves garlic, minced

1 medium carrot, diced small

3 stalks celery, thinly sliced

1 tsp tomato paste

1 tsp brown sugar

2 tbsp (30 ml) white wine

1 (14-oz (400-g)) can diced tomatoes

2 bay leaves

Salt

Pepper

BEETROOT SALAD

Wash the beets and place in a pot with enough water to cover them. Bring to a boil over high heat, then lower the heat to medium and cook until the beets are firm but cooked through, about 45 to 50 minutes. Drain and rinse the beets under cold running water. Remove the skin with your fingers or a vegetable peeler. Set them aside and let them cool down more.

When the beets are cool, slice them into chunks and place them in a large bowl, together with the remaining ingredients. Toss together, cover the bowl and refrigerate before serving.

3 medium fresh beets, trimmed

2 tbsp (30 ml) extra-virgin olive oil

1 tbsp (15 ml) red wine vinegar

1 clove garlic, minced

1 tbsp (4 g) chopped fresh parsley

Salt

Pepper

SPAGHETTI CARBONARA

This pasta dish is an Italian favorite. It actually used to be my favorite pasta dish in pre-vegan times, and I didn't eat it for so many years until I created my own version. Traditionally, carbonara is loaded with heavy cream and bacon. For a healthier plant-based alternative, in this recipe we make "bacon" out of edible rice paper sheets and use cashew cream instead of dairy cream. It is indulgent and delicious, yet so easy to prepare, and is definitely a staple dish in my home.

Serves 2 to 3

First make the rice paper bacon. Preheat the oven to 350°F (175°C). Line a baking sheet with parchment paper.

Take the rice paper sheets, stack them one on top of the other, and use kitchen scissors to cut them into strips. Set aside. To make the bacon marinade, in a small bowl add the oil, soy sauce, nutritional yeast, maple syrup, paprika, pepper, garlic powder and 2 tablespoons (30 ml) of warm water. Mix well. Add some warm water to a medium bowl and place it next to the bowl with the bacon marinade.

Take two rice paper strips, press them onto each other, and dip them in the warm water until they become slightly soft. Next, dip the double strip into the marinade and place it on the baking sheet. Repeat this process until all the strips are prepared. Use a pastry brush to brush any remaining marinade on the strips. Bake for 5 to 7 minutes. Make sure to check the strips often, as they burn very quickly. Once crispy, take them out of the oven and let them cool.

Make your carbonara sauce by adding all the ingredients to a blender or food processor and blending until it's smooth and creamy.

Cook the spaghetti al dente, according to the package instructions. Drain the cooked pasta and return it to the pot. Pour in the sauce and stir until the pasta is well-coated. Break up the bacon strips into little bits and add them to the pasta. Top with parsley.

Rice Paper Bacon Bits

2 rice paper sheets
1 tsp extra-virgin olive oil
1½ tbsp (22 ml) soy sauce
2 tbsp (10 g) nutritional yeast
½ tsp maple syrup
½ tsp smoked paprika or liquid smoke
Dash of black pepper
Dash of garlic powder

Carbonara Sauce

1 cup (150 g) raw cashews, soaked in water for at least 6 hours and drained
1 cup (240 ml) plant milk
½ tsp kala namak (black salt)
3 tbsp (15 g) nutritional yeast
3 to 4 cloves garlic
2 tsp (5 g) cornstarch
2 tbsp (30 ml) lemon juice
½ tsp black pepper

To Serve

10.5 oz (300 g) spaghetti
Fresh parsley, chopped

HEARTY LASAGNA

I'm a real sucker for a good lasagna. It doesn't matter the season, a large dish of freshly made lasagna will always warm my heart. This Hearty Lasagna is the perfect combination of a rich vegetable tomato sauce layered with creamy tofu ricotta and topped with melty cheese. It's the ultimate comforting and satisfying dinner for the whole family.

Serves 6

To make the ricotta, place all the ingredients, plus ¼ cup (60 ml) of water, in a high-speed blender and blend 1 to 2 minutes, until smooth. Transfer the ricotta to a bowl and set aside.

To make the vegetable filling, place the oil into a large pan over high heat. Add the onion and sauté for 2 to 3 minutes, then add the garlic and sauté for another 1 minute. Add the celery, carrot and mushrooms and stir to combine. Lower the heat to medium and cook for 2 to 3 minutes, then add the zucchini, eggplant, spinach and marinara sauce. Bring to a light simmer, lower the heat and cook for another 10 to 15 minutes.

Preheat the oven to 400°F (200°C). Grease a 9 x 13–inch (23 x 33–cm) lasagna pan.

To make the lasagna, place a few spoonfuls of the vegetable filling in the bottom of the pan and spread it evenly over the pan. Add 3 lasagna noodles, top with one-third of the ricotta, then more vegetable filling, and repeat until all the ingredients have been used up. Place in the oven and bake for 30 minutes.

In the meantime, combine all the mozzarella ingredients, plus 1½ cups (360 ml) of water, in a high-speed blender and blend for 1 to 2 minutes. Pour the mixture into a medium saucepan and place over medium heat. Cook for 60 to 90 seconds, stirring continuously, as the mozzarella firms up and gets stretchy. Remove from the heat, pour into a glass jar, cover and place in the fridge to chill.

After 30 minutes of baking, take the lasagna out of the oven and quickly spread spoonfuls of the mozzarella on top until you have used it all up. Immediately return the lasagna to the oven and bake for another 10 minutes. Turn the oven to broil and broil for 5 minutes, so the cheese is melted and bubbly. Take the lasagna out of the oven and let it cool down a bit before topping with fresh basil and serving.

Cashew Tofu Ricotta

1 cup (150 g) raw cashews, soaked in water overnight and drained

14 oz (400 g) silken tofu

⅓ cup (30 g) nutritional yeast

2 tbsp (30 ml) lemon juice

1 tsp garlic powder

½ tsp salt

Dash of black pepper

Vegetable Filling

2 tbsp (30 ml) extra-virgin olive oil

1 medium white onion, chopped

4 cloves garlic, minced

2 stalks celery, diced

1 medium carrot, chopped

8 oz (225 g) baby bella mushrooms, chopped

1 small zucchini, chopped

1 small eggplant, chopped

3 cups (90 g) baby spinach

2 (24-oz (680-g)) jars marinara sauce

9 no-boil lasagna noodles

Mozzarella

¼ cup (35 g) raw cashews

2 tbsp (30 ml) refined melted coconut oil

2 tbsp (10 g) nutritional yeast

1 tsp lemon juice

1 tsp apple cider vinegar

1 tsp agar powder

2½ tbsp (25 g) tapioca starch

½ tsp salt

Pinch of ground nutmeg

Topping

Fresh basil

LAYERED RATATOUILLE

Ratatouille always brings back very dear childhood memories for me. When I was growing up, we used to spend our summer vacations in France, and ratatouille is an easy but delicious and healthy dish that my mother used to make often, and still does to this day. This layered version of the famous French vegetable dish comes together quickly for a tasty weeknight dinner. Packed with delicious veggies and fresh herbs, it is the perfect main dish or part of any mezze.

Serves 4

Make the herb marinade by simply whisking all the ingredients together in a small bowl. Set aside.

To make the ratatouille, add the oil to a 9-inch (23-cm) ovenproof skillet and place over high heat. Add the onion and sauté for 3 to 4 minutes, then add the garlic and sauté for another minute. Add the red and yellow peppers and cook for 5 minutes, then add the diced roma tomatoes and cook for another 15 to 20 minutes over medium heat until they are broken down. Add the crushed tomatoes, red wine, basil and thyme, and season with salt and pepper. Let the ratatouille simmer for another 10 minutes. Taste and adjust the seasoning.

Preheat the oven to 400°F (200°C).

Arrange the sliced eggplants, zucchini and tomatoes in alternating patterns on top of the sauce right in the skillet, working from the outer edge to the middle of the pan. Season with salt and pepper. Brush the marinade over the vegetables, making sure to coat all the visible sides of the veggies. Cover the skillet with foil and bake for 40 minutes. Remove the foil, then bake for another 20 minutes, until the vegetables are softened. Serve with fresh basil on top.

Note: For best results, use a mandoline to make sure all the vegetable slices are the same thickness.

Herb Marinade

2 tbsp (30 ml) extra-virgin olive oil
1 tsp fresh thyme
2 tbsp (5 g) chopped fresh basil
1 tsp lemon juice
1 tbsp (15 ml) balsamic vinegar
Dash of coarse salt
Dash of black pepper

Ratatouille

2 tbsp (30 ml) extra-virgin olive oil
1 large red onion, diced
3 cloves garlic, minced
1 red bell pepper, stemmed, seeded and thinly sliced
1 yellow bell pepper, stemmed, seeded and thinly sliced
6 ripe roma tomatoes, diced small
1 (28-oz (800-g)) can crushed tomatoes
¼ cup (60 ml) red wine
1 tsp dried basil
1 tsp dried thyme
Salt
Pepper
3 medium eggplants, stemmed and sliced to ¼ inch (5 mm) thin
2 medium zucchini, sliced to ¼ inch (5 mm) thin
6 ripe roma tomatoes, sliced to ¼ inch (5 mm) thin

Topping

Fresh basil

SPAGHETTI BOLOGNESE

This is my take on the Italian classic. A flavorful bolognese sauce is a must-have in any kitchen, and this one has quickly become our go-to recipe at home. If you've had bad vegan bolognese before, this recipe will change your mind. It's rich, slightly sweet and full of flavor.

Serves 4

Make the Parmesan first. Place all the ingredients in a high-speed blender and pulse eight to ten times. Be careful not to blend too much, as you don't want it to become a nut butter. Place the mixture in a jar and set aside.

To make the bolognese, place the oil in a large saucepan over high heat. Add the onion and sauté for 2 to 3 minutes, until it's golden brown. Add the garlic and sauté for another 1 to 2 minutes. Use your hands to break the tofu apart into small crumbles and add them to the pan. Combine and sauté everything for 2 to 3 minutes. Add the mushrooms, walnuts, carrot and oregano and combine. Cook over medium heat for 3 to 4 minutes, until the mixture turns golden brown, then mix in the tomato paste. Slowly add the red wine and let the mixture simmer for 5 minutes, until the liquid has evaporated. Then add in the passata, salt, pepper and paprika and combine. Let the mixture cook for another 5 minutes, then add the pine nuts and basil.

Prepare the spaghetti according to the instructions on the box. Drain and put it back in the pot. Drizzle with a little olive oil so it won't be sticky, then add the bolognese and mix well. Top with the vegan Parmesan, fresh basil and grape tomatoes.

Parmesan

½ cup (72 g) blanched almonds
2 tbsp (10 g) nutritional yeast
1 tsp Himalayan salt
1 tsp garlic powder
1 tsp onion powder

Bolognese

3 tbsp (45 ml) extra-virgin olive oil
1 medium white onion, diced
3 cloves garlic, minced
14 oz (400 g) tofu
4 to 5 mushrooms, diced
½ cup (60 g) chopped walnuts
1 medium carrot, grated
1 tbsp (4 g) dried oregano
⅓ cup (80 g) tomato paste
⅔ cup (160 ml) red wine
28 oz (800 g) tomato passata (purée)
1 tsp salt
½ tsp black pepper
1 tsp sweet paprika
⅓ cup (45 g) pine nuts, roasted
1 cup (45 g) chopped fresh basil

To Serve

14 oz (400 g) spaghetti
Extra-virgin olive oil
Fresh basil
Halved grape tomatoes

LENTIL MOUSSAKA

Moussaka wasn't a dish I was familiar with until I moved to Cyprus. After tasting a deliciously smooth and rich moussaka from a local vegan restaurant a few years ago, I just had to re-create my own version. In this Lentil Moussaka, a scrumptious tomato-lentil sauce with a fragrant pinch of nutmeg and cinnamon is nestled between layers of roasted eggplant and potato and topped with a creamy béchamel sauce. It's the perfect healthy and hearty weeknight dinner.

Serves 6

Preheat the oven to 400°F (200°C). Line two baking sheets with parchment paper.

Arrange the potato and eggplant slices in a single layer on the baking sheets and brush them lightly with the olive oil. Sprinkle with salt and bake for about 30 minutes, flipping once about halfway through. Take them out of the oven and set aside to cool.

While they're cooking, make the filling. Heat the olive oil in a large skillet over medium heat. Add the onion and sauté for 2 to 3 minutes, then add the garlic and sauté for another minute. Add the carrot, salt, pepper, paprika, cinnamon and tomato paste and cook for 2 to 3 minutes, until the mixture is fragrant. Then add the diced tomatoes, lentils and bay leaves and bring to a simmer. Simmer over low heat for about 5 minutes. Remove the bay leaves and set the filling aside.

To make the béchamel, place the butter in a medium skillet over medium heat until it melts. Add the flour and whisk together. Cook for 1 minute, then add the cream and soy milk, whisking continuously to avoid lumps. Mix in the nutritional yeast, salt and nutmeg and whisk together until the mixture is smooth. Bring to a boil, then simmer over low heat for 2 to 3 minutes, until it thickens. Whisk continuously while it's cooking and remove from the heat as soon as it's done.

Grease a 9 x 13–inch (23 x 33–cm) baking dish. Arrange half of the potato and eggplant slices on the bottom of the baking dish. Top with all the lentil mixture, followed by the remaining potato and eggplant slices. Pour the béchamel on top and spread evenly. Bake for about 30 minutes or until the top is golden brown. Let it cool down slightly before topping with parsley and serving.

Vegetables

5 large potatoes, peeled and sliced to ½ inch (1 cm) thick

3 large eggplants, stemmed and sliced to ¾ inch (2 cm) thick

3 tbsp (45 ml) extra-virgin olive oil

½ tsp coarse salt

Filling

2 tbsp (30 ml) extra-virgin olive oil, plus more for greasing the pan

1 large white onion, chopped

3 cloves garlic, minced

1 large carrot, finely chopped

1 tsp salt

¼ tsp pepper

1 tsp sweet paprika

¼ tsp cinnamon

1 tsp tomato paste

1 (28-oz (800 g)) can diced tomatoes

¾ cup (150 g) cooked green lentils, rinsed and drained

2 bay leaves

Béchamel

3 tbsp (42 g) vegan butter

2½ tbsp (20 g) all-purpose flour

1 cup (240 ml) plant-based cream (soy or oat)

1 cup (240 ml) unsweetened soy milk

1 tbsp (5 g) nutritional yeast

½ tsp salt

Pinch of ground nutmeg

Topping

Chopped parsley

FRENCH CRÊPES

Ever since I was a child I have absolutely loved crêpes. Every year during our family's summer vacation in France, I'd indulge in those thin dough layers filled with cinnamon sugar. What can I say? I'm still in love, and this vegan version of the classic is as easy as it is delicious.

Serves 2

Place all the batter ingredients in a blender and blend on high speed for 30 seconds. Transfer to a bowl and set aside. You can also whisk the batter manually in a large bowl; just make sure to avoid lumps.

Lightly oil a nonstick pan and heat it over medium-high heat. Scoop about ¼ cup (60 ml) of the batter onto the pan, then rotate the pan to spread the batter out as thinly as possible. Cook the crêpe on each side for 40 to 50 seconds. Repeat with the rest of the batter.

Serve with your favorite toppings.

Note: I recommend rubbing the oil onto the pan with some paper towels to avoid having oily crêpes.

Batter

1 cup (125 g) all-purpose flour

1 tbsp (12 g) coconut sugar

1½ to 1⅔ cups (360 to 400 ml) almond milk

2 tbsp (30 ml) vegetable oil, plus more for greasing

½ tsp vanilla extract

Pinch of cinnamon

Pinch of salt

Toppings (optional)

½ tsp cinnamon

1 tsp granulated sugar (or any sugar you like)

Fresh fruits (such as figs, berries)

½ cup (140 g) coconut yogurt

Slivered almonds

Chopped pistachios

CRÈME BRÛLÉE

This vegan version of the French classic will make your heart jump. It is perfectly sweet, silky smooth and ultra creamy. It is also simple, fast and will make you crave more—guaranteed. Don't forget the blowtorch!

Serves 4

Set out four ramekins.

Place the coconut milk, almond milk, butter, tapioca, agar, turmeric, vanilla and 2 tablespoons (30 g) of sugar in a blender and blend until smooth, 30 to 60 seconds. Pour the mixture into a medium pan and place it over medium heat. Whisking frequently, cook the mixture until it's thickened, 5 to 8 minutes. You'll know it's ready when it's thickened significantly and is a smooth, creamy texture, similar to pudding.

Divide the mixture among the ramekins and knock them a few times on a countertop to even everything out and break up any air bubbles. Set them aside to cool to room temperature, then transfer them to the fridge to firm up for 4 to 6 hours.

When you're ready to serve, sprinkle 1 tablespoon (15 g) of sugar on each ramekin. Use a blowtorch to caramelize the top. If you don't have a blowtorch, you can put the sugar-dusted crème brûlées under the broiler on the top rack of your oven for 3 to 5 minutes.

Note: Only caramelize the crème brûlées right before serving, because the sugar will soften soon afterward.

1 (14-oz (400-ml)) can full-fat coconut milk

1 cup (240 ml) almond milk

1 tbsp (14 g) vegan butter, melted

2 tbsp (15 g) tapioca starch

¾ tsp agar powder

Pinch of turmeric

1 tsp vanilla extract

6 tbsp (90 g) sugar, divided

PASTEL DE NATA

These deliciously sweet custard-filled tarts are one of my favorite travel memories of Lisbon. Ever since I was little I've had a dear obsession with custardy pastries. Traditionally, custard is made with eggs and butter, but you won't miss them in this recipe. Perfectly creamy on the inside and surrounded by flaky pastry layers, these small bites of heaven will teleport you straight to Lisbon.

Serves 6

Defrost the puff pastry to room temperature. Grease a six-cup muffin tin with vegan butter. Lightly flour a work surface and spread out the puff pastry. With a floured rolling pin, roll the dough out as much as you can until it bounces back. Cut it into six equal pieces and press each piece into the muffin tin, down and up the sides and a little bit beyond the top. Place the cups into the fridge. In a small bowl, combine the sugar and cinnamon and set aside.

Preheat the oven to 450°F (230°C).

To make the filling, in a small saucepan over medium heat, heat 1 cup (240 ml) of the soy milk with the sugar and turmeric until it slightly simmers, 30 to 40 seconds. Whisk constantly while it comes to a simmer, making sure the sugar has dissolved, then take the pan off the heat. In a small bowl, combine the remaining ½ cup (120 ml) of milk with the cornstarch and vanilla powder and add it to the saucepan. Place the pan back over medium heat and bring it to a light boil, stirring continuously to avoid lumps, and simmer until you have a relatively thick mixture, about 2 to 3 minutes.

Take the muffin tin out of the fridge and scoop 2 to 3 tablespoons (30 to 45 ml) of the pudding mixture into each lined cup. Make sure not to overfill them and leave at least ¾ inch (2 cm) of space at the top. Sprinkle with a dash of the sugar and cinnamon mixture. Bake for 10 to 12 minutes, then turn the oven to broil and broil for about 2 to 3 minutes more. Remove the tarts from the oven and let them cool down completely before removing them from the tin.

Sprinkle some powdered sugar and cinnamon on top and serve.

Crust
7 oz (200 g) frozen vegan puff pastry
1 tbsp (14 g) vegan butter
1 tbsp (8 g) all-purpose flour
½ tsp sugar
¼ tsp cinnamon

Filling
1½ cups (360 ml) soy milk, divided
¼ cup (50 g) sugar
Dash of turmeric
4 tbsp (32 g) cornstarch
⅛ tsp vanilla powder

Topping
1 tsp powdered sugar
¼ tsp cinnamon

THE MIDDLE EAST

Middle Eastern cuisine is not only blessed with interesting flavors and spice combinations, but is also extremely abundant in high-quality fresh produce and nutritious plant-based staples. It's sunny there, and that puts the shine on vegetables. In short, it's vegan paradise.

This chapter is all about healthy legumes made into rich and creamy dips, as well as slow-cooked or roasted vegetables oozing with flavor, deliciously combined with exciting spices that will tickle your taste buds. You'll find a combination of traditional, centuries-old dishes like Baba Ganoush (page 78), which are vegan by nature, and modern twists on Tel Aviv–style cuisine, including sabich (page 63), shakshuka (page 70) and oven-roasted cauliflower (page 59). Let me take you on a journey from the creamiest hummus (page 53) to the most savory Mushroom Shawarma (page 69), ending with a piece of freshly baked Kunefe (page 79).

CREAMY HUMMUS WITH THREE TOPPINGS

Hummus is not just hummus. Having lived in Israel for more than two and a half years, this is the first lesson I learned there. Hummus is prepared in many different countries in many different ways. Over the years I've silently become kind of a hummus snob, so supermarket hummus just doesn't do it anymore. Once you've tasted the rich, creamy, almost silken texture of Tel Aviv hummus it's impossible to go back to anything else. Hummus is incredibly nutritious and healthy, and the flavor profile can vary a lot. My favorite kind of hummus is Israeli-style hummus, prepared with tons of good tahini and lots of lemon, with a super creamy texture. Israeli hummus is usually eaten with a variety of toppings, including roasted pine nuts, mushrooms and tahini, which keep the hummus from getting boring.

Serves 4

Rinse the dried chickpeas and place them in a big bowl. Add enough water to cover the chickpeas twice and stir in the baking soda. Let them soak for at least 6 to 8 hours. Then drain the chickpeas, saving the soaking water in a large pot. Add another 1 to 2 cups (240 to 480 ml) of clean water to the pot with the soaking water, place over high heat and bring to a boil. When the water is boiling, add the chickpeas ½ cup (100 g) at a time with 30 seconds between each addition. Skim off any foam that builds up at the surface, until it stops forming. Boil the chickpeas uncovered over high heat for 15 minutes, then turn down the heat a little bit and continue cooking for 70 to 80 minutes, until the chickpeas are soft and nicely cooked. You might have to add some more water as it evaporates. Turn off the heat and set the pot aside to cool down completely. You can do this overnight.

Drain the chickpeas, but keep ⅓ cup (80 ml) of the aquafaba and set it aside. Also set aside some cooled chickpeas for the garnish, and add the rest to a food processor or a good blender. Add the salt (start with less, you can always add more) and black and white pepper and pulse for a few seconds. Add the lemon juice, aquafaba and ⅓ cup plus 2 tablespoons (110 ml) of water, and blend for 1 to 2 minutes, until it's really smooth. Add in the tahini and blend another minute. Taste test and add a little bit more salt, water or lemon juice, according to your taste and desired texture.

To serve, divide the hummus among four serving bowls. Use a spoon to spread it out and make swirls. Then top with cumin, paprika, parsley, the reserved cooked chickpeas and a drizzle of olive oil, and add your favorite toppings.

(continued)

Hummus

11.6 oz (330 g) dried chickpeas

Pinch of baking soda

⅔ tsp salt, plus more to taste

Dash of black pepper

Dash of white pepper

⅓ cup (80 ml) lemon juice, plus more to taste

⅓ cup (80 ml) aquafaba (chickpea cooking water)

8 oz (225 g) tahini

Toppings

Dash of ground cumin

Dash of sweet paprika

2 tbsp (8 g) chopped fresh parsley

A few whole cooked chickpeas

Drizzle of extra-virgin olive oil

PINE NUT TOPPING

Place a small pan over medium heat. Add the pine nuts and toast them in the dry pan for a few minutes, stirring almost constantly. Be careful not to burn them. They are done when they are golden brown but not burned, about 2 or 3 minutes.

¼ cup (34 g) pine nuts

TAHINI TOPPING

Mix all the ingredients together in a small bowl. Add a bit of water to make it thinner if the texture is too thick for your taste.

½ cup (140 g) prepared tahini (from Roasted Eggplant and Tahini, page 56)
3 tbsp (30 g) cooked chickpeas
1 red onion, peeled and quartered

Note: In many Middle Eastern countries, but especially Israel, hummus is eaten as a main dish for breakfast or lunch. It is a popular street food that is served with many different toppings.

MUSHROOM TOPPING

Pull each oyster mushroom apart lengthwise into two or three strings and place them in a medium bowl together with the sliced cremini mushrooms. Add 3 tablespoons (45 ml) of oil and the soy sauce, spice mix, garlic powder, onion powder and pepper. Massage the spices into the mushrooms with your hands.

Place a large sauté pan over medium-high heat and add the remaining 1 tablespoon (15 ml) of oil. When the oil is hot, add the mushrooms and sauté for 4 to 5 minutes, until crispy. Make sure to flip them regularly so they don't burn.

17.6 oz (500 g) oyster mushrooms

7 oz (200 g) sliced cremini mushrooms

¼ cup (60 ml) extra-virgin olive oil, divided

3 tbsp (45 ml) soy sauce or tamari

½ tsp barbecue spice mix

1 tsp garlic powder

1 tsp onion powder

Dash of black pepper

ROASTED EGGPLANT AND TAHINI

These roasted eggplant slices are the best example of the genius of Middle Eastern cuisine: simple ingredients, easy method, incredible outcome. No wonder we eat these little slices of heaven about two or three times a week in my household. Thick, juicy eggplant slices are perfectly roasted in the oven, then dipped in deliciously creamy tahini— are you drooling yet? I've always quite underestimated eggplants, until I discovered this amazing dish.

Serves 3

Preheat the oven to 350°F (175°C). Line a baking sheet with parchment paper.

Slice each eggplant lengthwise into three equal thick slices and place them on the baking sheet. Brush both sides with a generous amount of olive oil and sprinkle with salt. Roast for 25 minutes, turn the slices over and roast for another 20 to 25 minutes, until they're nice and brown on both sides. If they're not yet browned, put the slices under the broiler for 2 to 3 minutes on each side.

Prepare the tahini by simply whisking all the ingredients, plus ⅓ cup and 2 tablespoons (110 ml) of water, together in a medium bowl. Let the roasted eggplant slices cool down a bit, then serve them with the tahini sauce. They can also be stored in the fridge for 1 to 2 days and simply roasted for another few minutes on each side before serving.

Note: These roasted eggplant slices are the base from which to make delicious Baba Ganoush (page 78) and also go really well on top of a bowl of Creamy Hummus (page 53) or as a filling for pita.

Eggplant

3 medium eggplants, peeled
5 tbsp (75 ml) extra-virgin olive oil
1 tsp coarse salt

Prepared Tahini

⅓ cup (80 g) tahini
2 tbsp (30 ml) lemon juice
Salt
Black pepper
2 tbsp (8 g) chopped fresh parsley
1 clove garlic, minced (optional)

ZA'ATAR ROASTED CAULIFLOWER

The hot foodie trend of roasting the whole cauliflower started in Israel before many variations spread worldwide. Seems simple, tastes incredible! You'll never underestimate cauliflower again after biting into a soft but crispy piece. This za'atar roasted version elevates the dish to another level, adding some exciting spices and flavors.

1 medium head cauliflower

2 tbsp (30 ml) extra-virgin olive oil

½ tsp coarse salt

1 tsp za'atar (see Note)

Serves 2 to 3

Preheat the oven to 450°F (230°C). Line a baking sheet with parchment paper.

Wash the cauliflower and take off the leaves. Cut out three-quarters of the stem and core, leaving just enough so the cauliflower stands upright. Fill a large pot with enough water to cover the whole cauliflower, place it over high heat and bring to a boil. When the water is boiling, carefully add the cauliflower and cook for 5 to 7 minutes (5 minutes if the cauliflower is smaller, 7 minutes if it is bigger).

Use a pair of tongs to carefully remove the cauliflower from the pot. Let it drain for a few seconds and then place it stem down on the baking sheet. Brush with olive oil, sprinkle with salt and za'atar, and roast for 25 to 30 minutes, until it's soft on the inside and crispy (but not too burnt) on the outside. Stick a fork into the stem to check if it's done. If it's not well browned, put the cauliflower under the broiler for about 5 minutes. Let it cool down a bit before serving.

Note: Za'atar is a dried spice mixture that typically includes oregano, thyme and sometimes other herbs, along with toasted sesame seeds, dried sumac, often salt, as well as other spices. You can find it in any Turkish or Arab grocery store or online.

CASHEW LABNEH

Labneh is a tangy, thick and creamy strained yogurt cheese from Lebanon. It is traditionally made from camel or goat milk, and is extremely addictive. Whenever I'd go to the north of Israel close to the Lebanese border, we would stop at one of the many Druze stands where friendly grandmothers would sell the most delicious labneh laffa (flatbread). This vegan version combines soy and cashews, with a tangy lemon taste to imitate that sour flavor. Sprinkle with some za'atar and add it to your mezze table. Or serve it with Za'atar Flatbread (page 62).

Serves 2 to 3

Rinse the soaked cashews and place them in a high-speed blender. Add 1 cup (240 ml) of water and the soy milk, yogurt and salt, and blend for 1 to 2 minutes, until it's completely smooth. Transfer to a saucepan and place over medium heat for 30 to 40 seconds, stirring constantly. It should become hot but not boiling or bubbling. Take the pan off the heat and stir in the lemon juice and vinegar. Set aside and let rest for 30 minutes.

Place a fine-mesh sieve over a bowl and lay a piece of cheesecloth inside. Pour the cashew mixture into the cheesecloth, twist the top closed and secure it with a rubber band. Place a small bowl or plate on top and let the mixture drain for 8 to 10 hours. Add a heavier weight (such as a bowl or several plates) and let drain for another 8 hours.

At this point the mixture should have the texture of a thick, creamy yogurt. Place it in a medium bowl, add the nutritional yeast, salt and pepper, and combine. To serve, spread the labneh on a platter, drizzle with the olive oil and sprinkle za'atar on top.

1 cup (150 g) raw cashews, soaked in water 6 to 8 hours

½ cup (120 ml) unsweetened soy milk

½ cup (140 g) unsweetened soy yogurt

¼ tsp salt, plus more to taste

¼ cup (60 ml) lemon juice

1 tbsp (15 ml) apple cider vinegar

1 tsp nutritional yeast

Black pepper

2 tbsp (30 ml) extra-virgin olive oil

1 tbsp (5 g) za'atar

ZA'ATAR FLATBREAD

Ever since someone handed me a warm flatbread right out of a wood-fired oven, I've been in love. And what better to dip into the creamy Cashew Labneh (page 60) than this deliciously fluffy manoushe—flatbread spiced with tons of za'atar? It is the perfect snack—warm, slightly supple dough slathered with za'atar, an herbaceous seasoning blend punctuated with sumac and sesame seeds.

Serves 6

Combine 1 cup (240 ml) of lukewarm water with the yeast and sugar in a small bowl. Set aside to rest for 10 minutes. Grease a large glass bowl with some olive oil and set it aside.

Place the flour and salt in a big bowl and make a well in the middle, then add the oil and the yeast mixture. Use a wooden spoon to combine the dough, then use your hands. Transfer the dough to a lightly floured work surface and knead for 5 to 10 minutes, until it is just slightly sticky. Place it in the greased glass bowl, cover with a towel, and let it rise in a warm place for 1½ hours.

While the bread is rising, prepare the za'atar oil by mixing everything together in a small bowl. Set aside.

Preheat the oven to 500°F (260°C). Line two baking sheets with parchment paper.

Place the dough on a floured surface and knead for another minute. Divide it into six equal parts. Use a rolling pin to roll each part out into a circle (just until the dough stretches back). Spread the circles on the baking sheets and generously brush the tops with the za'atar oil, leaving a ¾-inch (2-cm) rim around the edges. Bake for 8 to 10 minutes, until the tops are golden brown. Let cool for a few minutes and enjoy immediately.

*See photo on page 61.

Flatbread

1 tsp active dry yeast

1 tsp sugar

1 tsp extra-virgin olive oil, plus more for greasing

2⅔ cups (325 g) all-purpose flour, plus more for kneading

1 tsp salt

Za'atar Oil

⅓ cup (80 ml) extra-virgin olive oil

1 tbsp (5 g) za'atar

½ tsp coarse salt

SABICH WITH VEGAN "EGG"

Sabich might be the best invention since filled pitas. There is nothing better than walking back from the Tel Aviv beach on a hot summer day and stopping at your favorite sabich place to get your fix. This traditionally Iraqi-Jewish dish oozes with flavor. It combines everything I love about Middle Eastern cuisine: fluffy pita, hummus, tahini, roasted eggplants, potatoes, tons of fresh Arabic salad and amba—delicious pickled mango. Usually it is served with half a hard-boiled egg on top; so as not to miss out on the fun, you can find a vegan version in this recipe.

Serves 4

To make the vegan egg whites, combine all the ingredients, plus ½ cup (120 ml) of water, in a blender and blend until smooth. Pour the mixture into a small pot over medium heat and bring to a boil. Let it simmer while stirring for 60 seconds, then pour it into four half-egg molds and place them in the fridge for 1 to 2 hours to firm up.

While the egg whites are chilling, make the egg yolks. Place the cooked potato in a medium bowl and mash it with a fork. Add the butter, nutritional yeast, kala namak, turmeric and garlic powder and mix well.

Once the egg whites have firmed up, use a small melon scoop or a spoon to remove a half-circle indentation from each egg white. Place ½ teaspoon of the yolk mixture into each indentation and even it out. Place the "eggs" back into the fridge for 30 minutes.

Preheat the oven to 350°F (175°C). Line two baking sheets with parchment paper.

To make the roasted eggplants, place the eggplant slices on a baking sheet and brush both sides with olive oil and sprinkle with salt. Bake for 40 to 45 minutes total, flipping them over after 20 minutes of cooking time. If they're still not well browned, put the slices under the broiler for about 2 to 3 minutes on each side.

(continued)

Vegan Egg Whites

2 oz (60 g) silken tofu
1 tsp agar powder
1 tsp nutritional yeast
¼ tsp kala namak (black salt)

Vegan Egg Yolks

1 small white potato, peeled and boiled until soft
2 tsp (10 g) vegan butter
1 tsp nutritional yeast
⅛ tsp kala namak
½ tsp ground turmeric
¼ tsp garlic powder

Roasted Eggplants

2 medium eggplants, peeled and cut into 3 to 4 slices lengthwise
5 tbsp (75 ml) extra-virgin olive oil
1 tsp coarse salt

SABICH WITH VEGAN "EGG" (CONTINUED)

While the eggplants are roasting, make the roasted potatoes. Place them in a small pot and add enough water to cover. Boil them over high heat for 5 minutes, then drain. Place the potatoes in a small bowl, add the oil, salt and paprika, and mix. Place the potatoes on the second baking sheet and add them to the oven after you flip the eggplants. Bake for 15 to 20 minutes, until the potatoes are crispy.

When the potatoes and eggplant are done, assemble the sabich. Slice the vegan eggs. Cut one-quarter off the end of each pita and carefully create an opening. Add layers of prepared tahini, Creamy Hummus, Arabic Salad, roasted eggplant, roasted potatoes, amba, spring onion, parsley and sliced vegan egg.

Note: Silicone half egg molds can usually be found in baking equipment shops or simply online. It's easiest to find them in the weeks before Easter.

Roasted Potatoes

2 medium white potatoes, peeled and cut into wedges

2 tbsp (30 ml) extra-virgin olive oil

½ tsp salt

½ tsp sweet paprika

To Serve

4 pita breads

1 cup (280 g) prepared tahini (from Roasted Eggplant and Tahini, page 56)

½ cup (120 g) Creamy Hummus (page 53)

1 cup (160 g) Arabic Salad (page 77)

4 tbsp (85 g) amba

2 tbsp (8 g) spring onion, chopped

Chopped parsley

ROASTED PEPPER SALAD

This delicious salad has been a part of many cherished memories and celebrations during my travels in Israel. It is hands down the most delicious side salad or bread topping. Caramelized peppers roasted to perfection, combined with a dash of lemon, garlic and cilantro, will certainly create an explosion of flavors in your mouth and leave you wanting more! Serve on a piece of bread with prepared tahini (from Roasted Eggplant and Tahini, page 56) and enjoy.

Serves 3 to 4

8 medium red bell peppers

3 cloves garlic, minced

3 cloves garlic, sliced

2 tbsp (30 ml) lemon juice

1 tbsp (15 ml) balsamic vinegar

½ tsp dried thyme

⅓ cup (5 g) chopped fresh cilantro

¼ tsp salt

⅛ tsp black pepper

Preheat the oven to 350°F (175°C). Line a baking sheet with parchment paper.

Place the bell peppers, whole, on the baking sheet and roast for 40 to 45 minutes, rotating them a quarter turn every 10 minutes. If the skin is still not charred, put the pan under the broiler for about 5 minutes. Transfer to a pot with a tight-fitting lid and let them sweat while cooling down completely. Once cool, use your hands to remove the skin, core and seeds.

Place the soft flesh on a cutting board and chop a few times lengthwise. Place the peppers in a medium bowl, add the remaining ingredients and combine. Store in the fridge for up to 4 days.

MUSHROOM SHAWARMA

This recipe is a combination of cuisines. In Thailand, I got inspired to use oyster mushrooms as a juicy meat alternative, and in Israel I learned to love the smell of shawarma. Combining the two creates a mouthwatering dish that is one of my most popular recipes among family and friends. Take a bite of the warm pita filled with creamy hummus, tahini, salad, tangy amba and crispy mushrooms, and fly to heaven!

Serves 3

Preheat the oven to 400°F (200°C). Line a baking sheet with parchment paper.

Prepare the mushrooms by pulling them apart into strings. (The bigger the strings, the chunkier the mushrooms—they shrink a lot while baking.) Place the mushroom strings in a large bowl and add the oil, soy sauce, spice mix, garlic powder, onion powder, paprika and pepper. Mix it all together with your hands and gently massage everything into the mushrooms, then evenly spread them out on the baking sheet. Bake for 30 to 40 minutes (stirring twice), until they're brown and crispy. The longer you bake them the less juicy they get, so you want to find a good balance between crispy on the outside and juicy on the inside.

When the mushrooms are done, remove the pan from the oven and let them cool down a bit. While you wait, warm your pitas for a few minutes in the oven.

When you're ready to eat, cut about a quarter off one end of each pita and carefully open it with your hands or a knife. Inside the pita, smother the two sides and bottom with the prepared tahini and Creamy Hummus, then layer in some Arabic Salad, shawarma, more tahini and hummus, shawarma, salad and a drizzle of amba on top.

Note: Amba is a pickled mango condiment that's particularly popular in Iraq, Saudi Arabia and Israel. Outside of the Middle East, amba can often be found in kosher or Indian grocery stores, where you might find it labeled as mango pickle. You can also find it online.

35 oz (1 kg) oyster mushrooms

4 tbsp (60 ml) extra-virgin olive oil

5 tbsp (75 ml) soy sauce

¾ tsp barbecue spice mix

1 tsp garlic powder

1 tsp onion powder

1 tsp sweet paprika

¼ tsp pepper

To Serve

3 pita breads

½ cup (140 g) prepared tahini (from Roasted Eggplant and Tahini, page 56)

½ cup (120 g) Creamy Hummus (page 53)

1 cup (160 g) Arabic Salad (page 77)

2 tbsp (42 g) amba (see Note)

ONE-POT SHAKSHUKA

Shakshuka is an easy, one-skillet healthy breakfast that is served in many parts of the Middle East and North Africa. This version features a hearty spiced tomato and pepper sauce, topped with a vegan egg. Serve it with warm pita or toasted sourdough bread and fresh herbs or bean sprouts.

Serves 2 to 3

To make the shakshuka, place the bell peppers and carrots in a food processor and pulse a few times until you have nice small pieces. Set aside.

Put the oil in a large skillet over high heat. Add the onion and sauté for 1 to 2 minutes, then add the garlic and fresh chili and sauté for another 30 to 40 seconds. Add the chili flakes, paprika, brown sugar, tomato paste, salt and pepper, and sauté for another minute until the mixture is fragrant. Turn the heat down to medium, add the tomatoes and cook for about 20 to 25 minutes, until the tomatoes have broken down completely. Then add the passata and cook for another 10 minutes.

While the tomatoes are cooking, prepare the vegan eggs. For the yolks, add all the ingredients to a blender and blend until smooth. Set aside. Do the same for the egg whites, adding 1 teaspoon of water, and set aside.

When the shakshuka is ready, use the back of a large spoon or a ladle to make two or three wells in the mixture. Add a few spoonfuls of the egg white into each well and top each with 1 teaspoon of the yolk mixture. Let it cook for about 5 to 10 minutes, until the eggs have firmed up. Serve with some toasted bread and sprouts.

Shakshuka

2 medium red bell peppers, stemmed and seeded

2 medium carrots, peeled

3 tbsp (45 ml) extra-virgin olive oil

1 large white onion, diced

4 cloves garlic, minced

½ tsp fresh sliced chili pepper

¼ tsp dried chili flakes

1 tsp sweet paprika

1 tsp brown sugar

1 tbsp (16 g) tomato paste

1 tsp salt

¼ tsp black pepper

4 tomatoes, diced

½ cup (112 g) tomato passata (purée)

Vegan Egg Yolks

2 oz (60 g) sweet potato, peeled and boiled until soft

1 tsp grapeseed oil

1 tsp nutritional yeast

1½ tbsp (10 g) tapioca starch

Pinch of kala namak

Vegan Egg Whites

2 oz (60 g) silken tofu

1 tsp tapioca starch

Pinch of kala namak

To Serve

2 to 3 slices toasted bread

Handful of alfalfa sprouts

MUJADARA

Mujadara is everything I love about home-cooked Middle Eastern food. This delicious signature dish is made of flavor-packed layers of rice and lentils with heaps of caramelized onions on top. It's nutritious and delicious and the perfect hearty meal. It also goes very well with a big side of deliciously creamy tahini.

Serves 4 to 5

Place the oil in a medium pot over high heat. Add the onion and sauté for 1 to 2 minutes, until it's golden brown. Add all the garlic and sauté for another minute. Then add the salt, cumin, cinnamon and coriander, and sauté for another minute until fragrant. Add the rice and lentils and sauté for another 30 seconds, then add 3½ cups (840 ml) of water. Bring to a boil, then reduce the heat to low and cook for 17 to 20 minutes. Check with a fork after 17 minutes to see if the rice and lentils are cooked.

In the meantime, in a large frying pan, place the oil over medium heat. Add the onions and sauté for 10 to 15 minutes, stirring often, until they're caramelized. When the mujadara is cooked, either mix the onions into it or serve them on top.

3 tbsp (45 ml) extra-virgin olive oil

1 large yellow onion, diced

3 cloves garlic, minced

3 cloves garlic, sliced

1 tsp salt

1 tsp ground cumin

1 tsp cinnamon

½ tsp ground coriander

1 cup (185 g) basmati rice, rinsed and drained

1 cup (190 g) green lentils, soaked in water 4 to 6 hours, then rinsed and drained

Caramelized Onions

2 tbsp (30 ml) extra-virgin olive oil

3 large onions, sliced

SPINACH CHEESE BOUREKAS

Bourekas are a kind of baked pastry that's popular in Sephardic Jewish and Israeli cuisine. You'll find them freshly made on every other corner of Tel Aviv, just waiting to be devoured. They are made in a wide variety of shapes, with a vast selection of fillings inside the flaky puff pastry. One bite of this spinach and almond cheese–filled version fresh from the oven and you'll surely be a fan.

Serves 8

For the almond cheese, put the almonds in a high-speed blender. Add the remaining ingredients, plus ½ to ¾ cup (120 to 180 ml) of water. Start with less water and slowly add more, depending on your desired consistency. Blend until creamy. Use a spatula to scrape down the sides. Transfer to a bowl and place in the fridge to chill.

Take the puff pastry out of the freezer and let it thaw for 10 minutes.

Heat the olive oil in a medium nonstick pan over medium heat and add the garlic. Sauté for 30 to 60 seconds, then add the spinach. Sauté for another minute until it's wilted. Place in a medium bowl and let it cool down a bit, then add four or five spoonfuls of the almond cheese and combine. Season with salt and pepper according to your taste.

Preheat the oven to 400°F (200°C). Line a baking sheet with parchment paper.

Spread out the puff pastry on a work surface and cut it into 4-inch (10-cm) squares. Set a small dish of water next to your work surface. Place about 1 to 2 teaspoons (5 to 10 g) of the cheese-spinach mixture on one side of one pastry square, toward the corner, then fold over the opposite corner so you have a triangle. Wet the edges of the pastry with water and use a fork to press them down and seal the bourekas. Place them on the baking sheet, brush the top with aquafaba or soy milk, and sprinkle some sesame seeds on top. Bake for 18 to 20 minutes, until they're golden brown. Let them cool down a bit and enjoy.

Almond Cheese

1½ cups (215 g) blanched almonds, soaked in water for 6 hours or overnight and drained

2 tbsp (10 g) nutritional yeast

3 tbsp (45 ml) lemon juice

1 tbsp (15 ml) apple cider vinegar

3 tbsp (45 ml) extra-virgin olive oil

1 clove garlic, peeled

1 tsp salt

½ tsp garlic powder

Bourekas

17.5 oz (500 g) frozen vegan puff pastry

1 tsp extra-virgin olive oil

3 cloves garlic, minced

7 oz (200 g) fresh spinach, chopped

Salt

Black pepper

Toppings

1 tbsp (15 ml) aquafaba or soy milk

1 tbsp (9 g) mixed black and golden sesame seeds

TABBOULEH AND ARABIC SALAD

Tabbouleh and Arabic Salad are a staple side dish you'll find on almost any breakfast or lunch table in the Middle East. The combination of fresh herbs, vegetables, lots of lemon and spices will awaken your taste buds and make you crave more.

Serves 2 to 3

To make the bulgur, rinse and drain it, and place it in a small bowl. Cover with boiling water and let it soak for 20 to 30 minutes, then drain and set it aside to cool.

Add the shallot, cucumber, parsley, mint, pomegranate, oil, sumac and lemon juice to a medium bowl, then mix in the cooled bulgur and combine. Season with salt and pepper.

To make the Arabic salad, in a large bowl toss all the ingredients. Combine until the vegetables are evenly coated. Serve immediately.

Note: Sumac is a popular Middle Eastern spice made from a red berry. It's a versatile seasoning that adds tartness and vibrant red color to a dish. If you can't find sumac, replace it with grated lemon zest mixed with a bit of salt and black pepper.

Tabbouleh

¼ cup (35 g) bulgur

1 small shallot, finely chopped

¼ cup (30 g) diced cucumber

½ cup (30 g) chopped fresh parsley

1 to 2 tbsp (6 to 11 g) chopped fresh mint

½ cup (85 g) fresh pomegranate seeds

2 tbsp (30 ml) extra-virgin olive oil

1 tsp ground sumac (see Note)

1 tbsp (15 ml) lemon juice

Salt

Black pepper

Arabic Salad

2 ripe tomatoes, diced small

1 medium cucumber, diced small

½ medium red onion, diced small

2 tbsp (8 g) chopped fresh parsley

1 tbsp (15 ml) lemon juice

1½ tbsp (22 ml) extra-virgin olive oil

Dash of ground cumin

Dash of black pepper

¼ tsp salt

BABA GANOUSH

Baba ganoush, which literally means "spoiled dad," is a rich and super tasty eggplant dip. Traditionally, the first step to making baba ganoush is to grill the eggplant whole over an open fire or in the flame of a gas stove. But for convenience I went for a third option, which is slow-roasting the eggplant in the oven. This dish is creamy, silky and flavor-packed with garlic, tahini and lemon juice. It's perfect to serve with homemade flatbread or as part of your mezze.

Serves 4

Preheat the oven to 350°F (175°C). Line a baking sheet with parchment paper.

Slice each eggplant lengthwise into three equally thick slices and place them on the baking sheet. Brush both sides with a generous amount of olive oil and sprinkle with salt. Add the garlic clove to the baking sheet and place it in the oven. Take the garlic clove out after 10 minutes and set aside. Roast the eggplants for 25 minutes, turn the slices over and roast for another 20 to 25 minutes, until they're brown on both sides. If they're not yet browned, put the slices under the broiler for 2 to 3 minutes on each side. Take the pan out of the oven and let the eggplant cool down a bit. Remove the skin from the garlic clove.

Place the eggplant in a food processor. Add the garlic, tahini, lemon juice, salt and pepper and blend until smooth. Blend less for a chunkier texture, more for a very smooth texture. Add more coarse salt, pepper and lemon juice according to your taste.

*See photo on page 76.

3 medium eggplants, peeled

5 tbsp (75 ml) extra-virgin olive oil

1 tsp coarse salt, plus more to taste

1 clove garlic, unpeeled

½ cup (140 g) prepared tahini (from Roasted Eggplant and Tahini, page 56)

1 tbsp (15 ml) lemon juice, plus more to taste

½ tsp salt

Dash of black pepper, plus more to taste

KUNEFE

Kunefe (sometimes spelled knafeh) is a sweet cheese pastry originally from Turkey that can be found all over the Middle East. It's considered to be one of the best Turkish desserts ever—and that's saying a lot! I used to be quite obsessed with this dish, as I have a weakness for anything sweet and cheesy. I still remember very vividly my hunt through Jerusalem's Old Town for the best kunefe. This vegan version tastes incredibly similar to the original, with crispy kadayif pastry soaked in sweet syrup, filled with a delicious melting cheesy filling. It's impossible to stop at one piece!

Serves 8

To make the sugar syrup, place ½ cup (120 ml) of water and the powdered sugar and rose water, if using, in a small pot over medium heat and bring to a boil. Let it simmer until the syrup is reduced and thickened, 5 to 8 minutes, then set aside to cool.

Preheat the oven to 350°F (175°C). Grease a 9-inch (23-cm) round baking pan.

Place the kadayif in a large bowl, add the melted butter and mix with your hands until it's coated. Add half the dough to the greased pan and press it in evenly so it covers the bottom of the pan.

To make the filling, add all the ingredients to your blender and mix until smooth. Pour it into a saucepan and place over medium heat. Bring the mixture to a light boil and whisk continuously for 30 to 60 seconds until it has thickened and is stretchy. Remove from the heat and pour it over the dough in the pan. Even the filling out with a spoon and let it sit for 5 minutes. Then spread the remaining half of the dough on top of the filling in an even layer. Try to cover any holes or blank spots with leftover broken kadayif pieces.

(continued)

Sugar Syrup

⅓ cup (40 g) powdered sugar

1 tbsp (15 ml) rose water (optional)

Dough

4 tbsp (57 g) vegan butter, melted, plus more for greasing

7 oz (200 g) fresh or frozen kadayif (see Note)

Filling

10.5 oz (300 g) silken tofu, drained

½ cup (70 g) cashews, soaked in water for 4 to 6 hours and drained

½ cup (120 ml) full-fat coconut milk

⅓ cup (80 ml) maple syrup

1 tbsp (5 g) tapioca starch

1 tsp psyllium husk

1½ tbsp (22 ml) lemon juice

¼ tsp vanilla powder

Pinch of salt

KUNEFE (CONTINUED)

Bake for 35 to 40 minutes, until the top is nicely browned. Remove from the oven and let it cool for 10 minutes before attempting to flip it out of the pan. This is easiest done by placing a plate over the baking pan and flipping it. Pour some or all of the sugar syrup on top (depending on how sweet you like it), top with the pistachios and serve while still warm.

Topping

2 tbsp (18 g) crushed unsalted pistachios

Note: Kadayif (also spelled kadaif or kataifi) is finely shredded phyllo dough. It's sold fresh, frozen or dried in packages, and looks like vermicelli noodles. You can find it in Middle Eastern, Turkish and Greek food markets, and online (you may need to search a bit on all three spellings). Fresh or frozen kadayif are best for this dish, but if all you can find is the dried version, it should be fine, since it gets soaked with the butter and sugar syrup. To be on the safe side, if you are using dried kadayif, add 2 extra tablespoons (28 g) of melted vegan butter to massage into the dough before you put the kadayif in the baking pan.

CHICKPEA TAHINI BLONDIES

These melt-in-your-mouth blondies take two of the ingredients that can be found in any Middle Eastern kitchen and combine them into a deliciously sweet indulgence. Tahini (the Middle Eastern version of peanut butter) and chickpeas not only go well together in hummus, but they create that perfectly rich texture and taste that make these blondies so mouthwatering!

Serves 8

Preheat the oven to 350°F (175°C). Line an 8 x 8–inch (20 x 20–cm) baking pan with parchment paper.

Place the chickpeas, tahini, maple syrup, vanilla, almond flour, coconut sugar, baking powder and baking soda in a food processor and pulse until you have a smooth batter. Transfer to a medium bowl and stir in the chocolate chips and dates (if you're adding them). Spread the batter evenly in the prepared pan. Bake for 25 to 30 minutes, until the edges are golden. They will firm up as they cool, so don't worry if they're on the softer side.

Remove the pan from the oven and cool the blondies in the pan for 15 minutes. Carefully remove the blondies, and cut them into bars.

14 oz (400 g) cooked chickpeas

⅓ cup (80 g) tahini

5 tbsp (75 ml) pure maple syrup

1 tsp vanilla extract

½ cup (50 g) almond flour

¼ cup (40 g) coconut sugar

½ tsp baking powder

½ tsp baking soda

⅓ cup (55 g) vegan chocolate chips

2 pitted Medjool dates, chopped (optional)

SUFGANIYOT (JELLY DONUTS)

Sufganiyah is a round jelly donut eaten in Israel and around the world on the Jewish festival of Hanukkah. Think warm, fluffy donuts filled with sweet strawberry jam and powdered sugar on top that covers your nose every time you take a bite! I have very fond memories of the sweet yeast smell that fills the streets of Tel Aviv during Hanukkah and people waiting in line in front of their favorite local bakery to grab a bunch. I actually grew up eating something similar in Germany during Carnival. Over the years I have indulged in numerous (it's impossible to just eat one) of these sweet dough delights filled with all kinds of tastiness. They are quite easy to veganize, too.

Serves 8

To make the donuts, in a small bowl combine the yeast, soy milk, ¼ cup (60 ml) of lukewarm water and 1 tablespoon (15 g) of sugar and let stand until it's foamy, about 10 minutes. Lightly grease a medium bowl with a little vegan butter.

In a medium bowl, whisk together the flour, salt and remaining 2 tablespoons (30 g) of sugar. Add the yeast mixture, applesauce and butter and beat until the dough is soft but not sticky, 3 to 5 minutes. On a floured surface, knead the dough until it's smooth and elastic, about 3 minutes. Place the dough in the greased bowl. Cover with a towel and let it rise in a warm place for about 1½ to 2 hours, until it's doubled in size.

Lightly flour a baking sheet. Punch down the dough and place it on a lightly floured surface. Knead the dough a few times, then use a rolling pin to roll it out to ⅓ inch (8 mm) thick. Use a 2½-inch (6-cm) cookie cutter or a glass to cut out rounds and transfer them to the floured baking sheet. Re-roll any remaining dough and repeat until it's all cut. Cover the baking sheet with a towel and let the rounds rise for 30 minutes.

In a large, heavy-bottomed pot, use a thermometer to make sure the oil measures 375°F (190°C). Spread out some paper towels on a wire rack. Working with two at a time, add the donuts to the hot oil. Fry for 45 to 50 seconds on each side, then remove them with a slotted spoon and place them on the wire rack. Repeat with the remaining donuts. Let them cool down on the rack.

When the donuts are cool, spoon the jam into a pastry bag fitted with the star nozzle tip. Pierce a hole in the side of each donut with the tip. Squeeze the jam inside to fill it. Sprinkle the powdered sugar on top.

Donuts

1 tbsp (12 g) active dry yeast

¼ cup (60 ml) lukewarm soy milk

3 tbsp (45 g) sugar, divided

1 tbsp (14 g) vegan butter, room temperature, plus more for greasing

1⅓ cups (165 g) all-purpose flour, plus more for kneading

Pinch of salt

1 tbsp (15 g) unsweetened applesauce

3 cups (720 ml) vegetable oil

Filling

3 tbsp (45 g) strawberry jam

1 tbsp (8 g) powdered sugar

COCONUT MALABI

This delicious coconut milk pudding is a popular Middle Eastern dessert with origins in ancient Persia. It is silky smooth and creamy, and is served topped with a tangy grenadine to counterbalance the sweetness.

Serves 3

To make the grenadine, place all the ingredients plus 3 tablespoons (45 ml) of water in a small pan over high heat. Bring to a boil, then reduce the heat to a light simmer. Simmer for 3 to 5 minutes, until the grenadine is reduced and thickened. Set aside to cool.

To make the malabi, place all the ingredients plus 7 tablespoons (100 ml) of water in a large bowl and whisk together. Pour into a medium pan and place over medium heat. Cook for 2 to 3 minutes, stirring continuously to avoid lumps, until it thickens. Take off the heat and divide the malabi among three serving glasses. Even them out and set aside to cool down to room temperature, then transfer to the fridge and chill for at least 2 to 4 hours.

Just before serving, pour 1 to 2 teaspoons (5 to 10 ml) of the grenadine over the malabi, then sprinkle with the pistachios and coconut.

Grenadine

¼ cup (60 ml) fresh pomegranate juice

3 tbsp (45 g) sugar

¼ tsp rose water

Malabi

10 oz (300 ml) full-fat coconut milk

¼ cup (30 g) powdered sugar

¼ cup (32 g) cornstarch

¼ tsp vanilla powder

½ tsp rose water

Toppings

2 tbsp (18 g) crushed unsalted pistachios

2 tbsp (12 g) shredded coconut

ASIA

Most Asian restaurants are a vegan's best friend; you'll find plenty of vegan dishes on the menu and will be sure to have a flavorful and satisfying meal. But there are also many popular and delicious dishes that are not vegan. Happily, they are easy to veganize.

In this chapter, you'll find a combination of delicious plant-based versions of my favorite Thai, Japanese, Indian and Vietnamese dishes. We're talking rich sesame ramen (page 94), street style pad Thai (page 97), mouthwatering sushi rolls (pages 93 and 98) and Matcha Ice Cream (page 122) that tastes just like the real thing.

SWEET POTATO TEMPURA ROLL

Making sushi rolls at home may seem like a lot of work, but it's actually a lot of fun. I love playing with different flavors and fillings, and this roll is one of my favorites. The crunchy sweet potato tempura on the inside is perfectly complemented by the smooth avocado coating on top.

Serves 2

Start with the rice. Place 13 ounces (385 ml) of water in a saucepan and add the rice. Place over high heat and bring to a boil, then turn the heat down to low, cover the pot and let the rice simmer for about 15 to 20 minutes. Remove from the heat and leave the rice to steam another 10 to 15 minutes without opening the lid. Then stir in the rice vinegar and carefully combine.

Preheat the oven to 350°F (175°C). Line a baking sheet with parchment paper. To make the sweet potato tempura, in a medium bowl combine the breadcrumbs, flour, paprika, garlic powder and salt and whisk together. Place the milk in a small bowl. Dip each sweet potato slice into the milk, then in the breadcrumb mixture, then milk again, then breadcrumb mixture again. Put it on the baking sheet and spray with a bit of oil. When all the sweet potato is breaded, bake it for 30 minutes, until the slices are crispy on the outside and soft on the inside.

To make the rolls, lay out the tempura, cucumber, carrot and avocados around your workspace. Cut the nori sheets in half. Take half a nori sheet and place it on a bamboo mat, shiny side down. Place a ½ cup (100 g) of the sushi rice on the nori and evenly spread it out and press down, leaving a ½-inch (1-cm) border all around the edges. You may need to wet your hands for easier handling. Cover the rice with plastic wrap and carefully turn the nori sheet over so the rice is facing down. On the lower third of the nori, add the cucumber, carrot, long slices of avocado and cooked sweet potato. Use the bamboo mat to roll the sushi up from the bottom into a tight roll. Remove the plastic wrap from the rice side. Now you have a roll with rice on the outside and veggies on the inside.

Take the short avocado slices and spread them along the top of the sushi roll, over the rice. Place a piece of plastic wrap over the top of the roll, over the avocado. Use the bamboo mat to gently press the avocado down to cover the top of the roll. Remove the plastic wrap and cut the roll into thick slices. Repeat with the other nori sheets.

Sushi Rice

7 oz (200 g) sushi rice, washed thoroughly, soaked in water for 30 minutes, and drained

⅓ cup (80 ml) rice vinegar

Sweet Potato Tempura

⅓ cup (18 g) panko breadcrumbs

¼ cup (31 g) all-purpose flour

½ tsp smoked paprika

½ tsp garlic powder

Pinch of salt

⅓ cup (80 ml) almond milk

1 medium sweet potato, peeled and sliced to ½ inch (1 cm) thick

1 to 2 tbsp (15 to 30 ml) vegetable oil, in a sprayer

Filling

1 medium cucumber, julienned

1 medium carrot, julienned

2 ripe avocados, 1 cut in long slices, 1 cut in short slices

3 to 4 sheets nori

Topping

Sesame seeds

GOLDEN SESAME RAMEN

As with many things, I never really had ramen until I tried ramen in Tokyo. During my travels through Japan I fell in love, not only with the country and its people, but specifically with the golden ramen from T's Tantan at Tokyo Station. At T's they make all the ramen types vegan, really succulent and perfectly spiced so that they resemble their meat counterparts. In an attempt to re-create those flavors, this ramen is a very close version of their delicious bowl of rich broth.

Serves 2 to 3

To make the tofu crumbles, place the tofu in a medium bowl and use your hands or a fork to break it apart into small crumbles. Combine the soy sauce, mirin and miso paste in a small bowl and whisk together. Place the oil in a small frying pan over medium-high heat. Add the tofu crumbles and stir-fry for 4 to 5 minutes, until golden, then add the sauce and stir-fry for another minute. Take off the heat and set aside.

Cook the ramen noodles according to the package instructions and set aside.

To make the broth, place 2 tablespoons (30 ml) of the sesame oil in a medium pot over medium heat. Add the garlic and ginger and stir-fry for 1 to 2 minutes, until golden. Add the vegetable broth and bok choy and cook on a light simmer for about 8 to 10 minutes, until tender. While it's cooking, in a small bowl whisk together the tahini, miso paste, soy sauce, sugar, remaining sesame oil and chili oil. Take the pot with the broth off the heat. Pour in the tahini mixture and soy milk and whisk together.

In each serving bowl, place a portion of ramen noodles, some broth, tofu crumbles and spring onion on top.

Tofu Crumbles

7 oz (200 g) firm tofu, drained

1½ tbsp (22 ml) soy sauce

1 tsp mirin

½ tsp miso paste

2 to 3 tbsp (30 to 45 ml) neutral-flavor oil

Ramen

4 portions ramen noodles

Broth

3 tbsp (45 ml) sesame oil, divided

5 cloves garlic, minced

2 tbsp (14 g) minced fresh ginger

4 cups (960 ml) vegetable broth

2 baby bok choy heads, washed, trimmed and sliced

½ cup (140 g) tahini

1 tsp miso paste

3 tbsp (45 ml) soy sauce

½ tsp sugar

1 tbsp (15 ml) chili oil

1 cup (240 ml) soy milk

Topping

6 spring onions, sliced

EASY TOFU PAD THAI

Pad Thai is one of the most popular Thai street foods and is served in Thai restaurants all over the world. The original version contains shrimp paste, fish sauce and eggs, but even without these ingredients, this vegan version still packs a flavor punch that comes very close to the vegan Pad Thai I've had in Thailand.

Serves 4

To make the sauce, in a small saucepan add the soy sauce, tamarind paste, brown sugar and 4 tablespoons (60 ml) of water. Heat over medium heat until they're just simmering. Cook for 1 to 2 minutes, until the sauce is reduced a bit, stirring occasionally, then turn off the heat. Whisk in the lime juice, chili flakes, sesame oil and rice vinegar and set aside.

Bring a large pot of water to a boil. Add the noodles and cook for 3 to 4 minutes less than it says on the package. Drain and rinse the noodles under cold water. Set aside.

Heat the sesame oil in a wok or a large skillet over high heat. Add the tofu and stir-fry for 3 to 4 minutes, until it's golden brown. Then add the garlic and spring onions and stir-fry for another 30 seconds. Add the carrot and stir-fry for 1 minute, then add the noodles, bean sprouts and the sauce, and continue to stir-fry for another minute. Transfer the pad Thai to a serving bowl. Top with the peanuts, lime juice and cilantro.

Sauce

¼ cup (60 ml) soy sauce

2 tbsp (25 g) tamarind paste

¼ cup (55 g) brown sugar

1 tbsp (15 ml) lime juice

½ tsp dried chili flakes

1 tsp sesame oil

1 tsp rice vinegar

Noodles

10.5 oz (300 g) pad Thai rice noodles

2 tbsp (30 ml) sesame oil

14 oz (400 g) firm tofu, drained and diced into ¾-inch (2-cm) cubes

2 cloves garlic, minced

5 spring onions, cut into 1-inch (3-cm) pieces

1 medium carrot, julienned

2 cups (208 g) mung bean sprouts

To Serve

¼ cup (37 g) roasted peanuts, chopped

Juice of 1 lime

2 tbsp (3 g) fresh chopped cilantro

EGGPLANT DRAGON ROLL

Traditional sushi chefs from Japan might roll their eyes when they see this kind of Western-style sushi, but that doesn't make it any less tasty. This vegan version of a dragon roll is coated with flavorful miso-roasted eggplant and a crunchy vegetable filling. Serve with soy sauce on the side, and don't forget the chopsticks.

Serves 2

Preheat the oven to 350°F (175°C). Line a baking sheet with parchment paper.

To make the miso eggplant, in a small bowl combine the sesame oil, miso paste, maple syrup and 2 tablespoons (30 ml) of hot water and mix until the miso paste is dissolved. Place the eggplant slices on the baking sheet and brush both sides with the marinade. Bake for 10 to 15 minutes, turn the slices over and bake for 10 to 15 minutes more (be careful not to let them burn). Take the pan out of the oven and set aside.

To make the rolls, lay out the miso eggplant, cream cheese, cucumber, carrot and avocado around your workspace. Cut the nori sheets in half. Take half a nori sheet and place it on a bamboo mat, shiny side down. Place a ½ cup (100 g) of the sushi rice on the nori and evenly spread it out and press down, leaving a ½-inch (1-cm) border around the edges. You may need to wet your hands for easier handling. Cover the rice with plastic wrap and carefully turn the nori sheet over so the rice is facing down. On the lower third of the nori, spread some cream cheese and add the cucumber, carrot and avocado. Use the bamboo mat to roll the sushi up from the bottom into a tight roll. Remove the plastic wrap from the rice side. Now you have a roll with rice on the outside and veggies on the inside.

Take the cooked eggplant slices and lay them side by side along the top of the sushi roll, over the rice. Place a piece of plastic wrap over the top of the roll, over the eggplant. Use the bamboo mat to gently press the eggplant down to cover the top of the roll. Remove the plastic wrap and cut the roll into thick slices. Repeat with the other nori sheets.

Miso Eggplant

2 tbsp (30 ml) sesame oil

1 tbsp (16 g) miso paste

2 tbsp (30 ml) maple syrup

2 long Asian eggplants, peeled and sliced into thin strips

Rolls

3 tbsp (45 g) vegan cream cheese

1 small cucumber, julienned

1 medium carrot, julienned

½ avocado, sliced lengthwise

3 to 4 nori sheets

7 oz (200 g) cooked sushi rice (prepared as for Sweet Potato Tempura Roll, page 93)

Topping

Sesame seeds

UDON SHIITAKE NOODLE BOWL

Dried shiitake mushrooms, seaweed and lots of garlic and ginger elevate this dish from a regular noodle soup to a crave-worthy meal that is bursting with flavor. Make sure to cook the noodles separately so they don't become mushy.

Serves 3

To make the broth, heat the oil in a large pot over high heat. Add the scallions and stir-fry for 1 to 2 minutes, then add the garlic and ginger and sauté for another 1 to 2 minutes. Add the leeks and cook for 2 to 3 minutes, then add the chopped shiitake mushrooms, seaweed, salt and 8 cups (2 L) of water. Bring to a boil, then reduce the heat to a low simmer. Let the broth simmer for 15 minutes. Add the bok choy and sliced shiitake mushrooms and simmer for 10 minutes more.

While the broth is simmering, cook the udon noodles according to the package instructions. Drain and rinse with cool running water, then drizzle with some sesame oil and set aside.

When the broth is done, take the pot off the heat. Add the mirin, miso paste, soy sauce and tofu to the broth and stir to combine. Place a portion of noodles into each serving bowl, pour in some broth and top with some chili flakes and spring onions.

3 tbsp (45 ml) sesame oil, plus more for the noodles

5 scallions, trimmed and diced

4 cloves garlic, minced

1 tbsp (7 g) fresh grated ginger

1½ cups (150 g) chopped leeks

½ cup (35 g) chopped dried shiitake mushrooms

⅓ cup (25 g) dried seaweed (flakes or crumbled)

1 tsp salt

3 cups (210 g) chopped bok choy

½ cup (35 g) sliced dried shiitake mushrooms

10.5 oz (300 g) udon noodles

4 tbsp (60 ml) mirin

⅓ cup (80 g) miso paste

1 tbsp (15 ml) soy sauce

14 oz (400 g) silken tofu, diced

Toppings

Dried red chili flakes

Sliced spring onions

PICKLED PLUM ONIGIRI

While traveling in Japan, I must have eaten around 20 umeboshi onigiri (rice balls) a week. They are available at every other 7-Eleven and grocery store, and once I had found a vegan brand I couldn't stop snacking on them. So simple, but the sour pickled plum taste is one of my favorite flavors.

Serves 2

Cut the pickled plums into cubes. Sprinkle a bit of salt into your hand and scoop up about ⅓ cup (60 g) of cooked rice. Mold the rice into a triangle with sides about 3 inches (7.5 cm) long. Use your finger to make a small well in the center of the rice and place some pickled plum inside. Mold the rice around the well with your hands to cover. Cut each nori sheet into three pieces and wrap the lower bottom side of each onigiri with one-third of a sheet, leaving one tip unwrapped. Sprinkle with sesame seeds.

> *Note:* Umeboshi is a pickled ume fruit (a kind of plum) common in Japan. You can find it whole or as a paste in most Asian grocery stores or online.

Handful umeboshi (pickled plums) or 5 tbsp (85 g) umeboshi paste (see Note)

Salt

7 oz (200 g) cooked sushi rice (prepared as for Sweet Potato Tempura Roll, page 93)

2 nori sheets

Sesame seeds

MISO EDAMAME SALAD

This quick and saucy dish, somewhere between a noodle bowl and a salad, is a combination of my favorite peanut-miso dressing and lots of fresh and nutritious ingredients. Don't be tempted to skimp on the mushrooms—they're a must for flavor and texture.

Serves 4

To make the dressing, in a medium bowl combine all the ingredients, as well as ¼ to ⅓ cup (60 to 80 ml) of warm water (depending on the consistency you like). Whisk together until it's smooth. Set aside.

Cook the soba noodles according to the package instructions. Drain and rinse under cool running water, then drizzle them with a little sesame oil and set aside.

To make the salad, heat the sesame oil in a medium skillet over medium-high heat. Add the garlic and ginger and stir-fry for 1 minute, then add the oyster mushrooms. Stir-fry for 2 to 3 minutes, until they're golden brown. Add the enoki mushrooms and stir-fry for another 20 to 30 seconds, then take the pan off the heat and set aside to cool.

Put the mushroom mixture and the noodles in a large bowl. Add the spring onions, carrot, red cabbage and edamame. Pour on the dressing and toss to coat everything. Sprinkle with sesame seeds and serve.

Peanut-Miso Dressing

¼ cup (65 g) peanut butter

2 tbsp (30 ml) lime juice

2 tbsp (30 ml) maple syrup

1 to 2 tbsp (15 to 30 ml) rice vinegar

1½ tbsp (22 g) miso paste

2 tbsp (30 ml) sesame oil

1 tbsp (15 ml) soy sauce

1 to 2 tsp (5 to 10 ml) chili sauce

Salad

10.5 oz (300 g) soba noodles

2 tbsp (30 ml) sesame oil, plus more for the noodles

3 cloves garlic, sliced

1 tbsp (7 g) grated fresh ginger

6 king oyster mushrooms, sliced

1 bunch enoki mushrooms

2 spring onions, sliced

1 medium carrot, julienned

¼ red cabbage, sliced

1 cup (156 g) frozen shelled edamame, cooked

Sesame seeds

SPICY "TUNA" MAKI

Did you know you can make vegan "tuna" from tomatoes? As crazy as it sounds, it's actually incredibly delicious. Slightly cooked tomato flesh soaked in a flavorful fishy marinade works miracles, especially in combination with the other flavors of sushi. You really can veganize anything!

Serves 2

To prepare the tomatoes, fill a small pot with water and bring it to a boil. Make four small cuts in the skin on the top of each tomato and place them in the pot. Boil for 40 to 60 seconds until the skin is beginning to lift off. Immediately take the pot off the heat, drain, and rinse the tomatoes with cold water to prevent further cooking. Use your hands to carefully peel off the skin. Quarter the tomatoes and use a melon or a spoon to scoop out the inner parts (seeds, liquids, etc.) until you have simple pieces of tomato left.

To make the marinade, in a medium bowl combine the soy sauce, miso paste, oil, liquid smoke, nori and chili sauce, as well as 2 tablespoons (30 ml) of hot water. Place the tomato pieces in the marinade and stir to cover all the pieces. Place in the fridge for 1 to 2 hours, or overnight.

To make the rolls, lay out all the prepared tomatoes and the cream cheese near your workspace. Cut the nori sheets in half. Take half a nori sheet and place it on a bamboo mat, shiny side down. Place ½ cup (100 g) of the sushi rice on the nori and evenly spread it out and press down, leaving a ½-inch (1-cm) border around the edges. You may need to wet your hands for easier handling. On the lower third of the rice, spread the cream cheese and add some tomato pieces. Use the bamboo mat to roll the sushi up from the bottom into a tight roll. Now you have a roll with rice on the inside and nori on the outside. Remove the bamboo mat and cut the roll into thick slices. Repeat with the other nori sheets. Serve with soy sauce and green onions.

"Tuna"

3 ripe roma tomatoes

1 tbsp (15 ml) soy sauce

1 tsp miso paste

1 tbsp (15 ml) extra-virgin olive oil

½ tsp liquid smoke

1 tsp nori flakes (see Note)

1 tsp chili sauce

Maki Rolls

3 tbsp (45 g) vegan cream cheese

3 to 4 nori sheets

7 oz (200 g) sushi rice (prepared as for Sweet Potato Tempura Roll, page 93)

To Serve

Soy sauce

Green onions

Note: For nori flakes, you can simply grate, chop or crumble a nori sheet.

RED CURRY

I remember being so impressed by the many vegan street food choices when I was in Bangkok, and red curry was one of my favorites. You can find red curry on every corner in Thailand. Now I make this delicious Red Curry about once a week, because it's just so simple, super nutritious and extremely tasty. The curry is loaded with fresh veggies and topped with deliciously crunchy fried tofu. If you want to go for an even healthier version, instead of frying the tofu, bake it at 400°F (200°C) for 25 to 30 minutes, tossing it halfway through the cooking time.

Serves 4

To make the tofu, place the cornstarch, salt and tofu in a small container, close with the lid, and gently shake to coat the tofu cubes. Line a plate with paper towels. Place the oil in a medium frying pan over medium-high heat and add the coated tofu. Stir-fry on all sides about 6 to 8 minutes until golden, then place on the lined plate and set aside.

To make the curry, place the coconut oil in a large pan over medium-high heat. Add the onion and sauté for 2 to 3 minutes, then add the garlic and ginger and sauté for another minute. Add the carrots, potato, curry paste and sugar and combine. Cook for 2 to 3 minutes, then add the coconut milk and 1 cup (240 ml) of water. Bring to a boil, then turn down the heat to a gentle simmer and cook for 10 to 15 minutes, until the potatoes are tender. Add the snap peas, soy sauce, salt, pepper and lime juice and cook for another 2 to 3 minutes. Finally, add the fried tofu, season with salt and pepper and combine.

Serve over cooked rice. Top with cilantro, lime juice and chili flakes.

Fried Tofu

¼ cup (32 g) cornstarch

⅛ tsp salt

14 oz (400 g) firm tofu, drained and diced

4 tbsp (60 ml) neutral-flavor oil

Curry

2 tbsp (30 ml) melted coconut oil

1 medium white onion, diced

4 cloves garlic, minced

1 tbsp (7 g) minced fresh ginger

2 medium carrots, diced small

1 medium russet potato, peeled and diced

2 tbsp (32 g) Thai red curry paste

1 tsp brown sugar

26 oz (770 ml) coconut milk

1 cup (100 g) snap peas

1 tbsp (15 ml) soy sauce

Salt

Pepper

1 tbsp (15 ml) fresh lime juice

To Serve

2 cups (372 g) cooked basmati rice

Handful of chopped fresh cilantro

Juice of ½ lime

½ tsp dried chili flakes

SEITAN LARB WITH PICKLED ONIONS

Larb is a type of meat salad eaten in Laos and Thailand. During the three months I spent in Thailand, I ate so many different vegan versions of larb that it became one of my go-to dishes. There are many ways to veganize it by using tofu, seitan or mushrooms instead of meat. This recipe uses seitan, which is wonderfully seasoned with soy sauce, lime juice and chili flakes. The pickled onions on top add lots of tangy sweetness to the savory larb.

Serves 3 to 4

To make the pickled onions, put 7 ounces (200 ml) of hot water and the salt into a glass jar and stir until the salt is dissolved. Add the remaining ingredients, close the lid and gently shake the jar a few times. Set aside for 6 to 8 hours, then transfer to the fridge.

To make the larb sauce, in a small bowl whisk together the soy sauce, lime juice and maple syrup. Set aside.

Place the sesame oil in a medium pan over medium-high heat. Add the shallots and stir-fry for 1 minute, then add the garlic, ginger, chili pepper and spring onions and stir-fry for another 2 to 3 minutes. Add the seitan to the pan and stir-fry for 3 to 4 minutes, then add the larb sauce and stir-fry for another 2 minutes. Take the pan off the heat, then mix in the mint and cilantro.

Spoon a few spoonfuls of the larb into each of the lettuce leaves, and garnish with the pickled onions, a squeeze of lime juice and some roasted peanuts, if desired.

Pickled Onions

½ tsp salt

1 medium red onion, thinly sliced

3.5 oz (100 ml) rice vinegar

3.5 oz (100 ml) apple cider vinegar

1 clove garlic, thinly sliced

2 tsp (6 g) whole peppercorns

Larb

2 tbsp (30 ml) soy sauce

2 tbsp (30 ml) lime juice

1 tbsp (15 ml) pure maple syrup

2 tbsp (30 ml) sesame oil

3 shallots, finely diced

3 cloves garlic, minced

1 tbsp (7 g) grated fresh ginger

1 fresh hot red chili pepper, thinly sliced

⅓ cup (34 g) sliced spring onions

7 oz (200 g) seitan, crumbled apart with your fingers

⅓ cup (32 g) chopped fresh mint

⅓ cup (6 g) chopped fresh cilantro

1 head lettuce, separated into leaves

Lime wedges (optional)

¼ cup (35 g) chopped roasted peanuts (optional)

SUMMER ROLLS WITH SPICY PEANUT SAUCE

This is the ideal light meal or snack for a warm summer day. It's one of the dishes I always order at any Vietnamese restaurant I go to, because I like it so much. During my Thailand travels, I ate summer rolls daily and became slightly addicted to them. These rolls are packed with fresh veggies and herbs, plus the creamiest spicy peanut sauce of your dreams. Get rollin' and dippin'!

Serves 2

Prepare all the ingredients for the summer rolls and arrange them on a work surface, so you have them right on hand when you are making the rolls.

Pour some hot water on a large plate with a rim. Take a rice paper sheet and soak it for about 10 seconds on each side, then remove it and place it on a clean work surface. Arrange the filling ingredients horizontally in the lower one-third of the sheet, starting with the lettuce and cilantro at the bottom of the sheet. Take just a bit of each filling but don't overfill, or the rice paper will tear. Fold the rice paper over the ingredients and tightly press them inside, pushing them toward you. Fold in the sides like a burrito, then continue to roll the paper up firmly until the end. Set it aside, seam side down. Continue with the remaining rice paper and filling. Don't cut the rolls right away; wait a bit until the rice paper firms up.

To make the spicy peanut sauce, in a small bowl combine all the ingredients, as well as 3 to 5 tablespoons (45 to 75 ml) of warm water (depending on the consistency you like). Adjust the spiciness, saltiness and sweetness according to taste.

Cut the summer rolls in half and serve with the sauce on the side.

6 sheets rice paper

Summer Rolls

2 cups (95 g) shredded romaine lettuce

1 cup (16 g) fresh cilantro leaves

1 medium cucumber, sliced

2 medium carrots, julienned

7 oz (200 g) smoked tofu, cut into strips

3 oz (80 g) rice noodles, cooked according to the package instructions and chopped

¼ red cabbage, shredded

1 ripe avocado, sliced

Spicy Peanut Sauce

3 tbsp (48 g) peanut butter

1 to 2 tbsp (15 to 30 ml) soy sauce

1 to 2 tsp (5 to 10 ml) lime juice

1 tsp maple syrup

1 tsp hot sauce, such as sriracha

RED LENTIL DHAL

This Red Lentil Dhal, or Masoor Dal, is bound to become one of your favorites. It's easy to make, incredibly nutritious, delicious and hearty. Serve with some vegan yogurt to balance the spiciness, and cooked basmati rice or garlic naan on the side.

Serves 4

Place the coconut oil in a large saucepan over medium-high heat. Add the onion and stir-fry for 3 minutes. Add the garlic and ginger and stir-fry for another minute. Then add the chili pepper, carrot and tomatoes and stir-fry for another 2 minutes. Stir in the cumin, coriander, mustard seeds, turmeric, garam masala, salt, pepper and paprika and stir-fry until they're fragrant, about 1 to 2 minutes. Add the lentils, 2½ cups (600 ml) of water and the coconut milk and combine. Bring to a boil and let the dahl simmer for 15 to 20 minutes, until it has reached a thick consistency. Add the spinach and cook for another 2 or 3 minutes.

To serve, top with lemon juice, chili flakes, cilantro and yogurt.

Dhal

2 tbsp (30 ml) melted coconut oil
1 large yellow onion, diced
5 cloves garlic, minced
1 tbsp (7 g) minced fresh ginger
1 fresh green chili pepper, sliced
1 medium carrot, diced small
10 cherry tomatoes, quartered
1 tsp ground cumin
¼ tsp ground coriander
½ tsp mustard seeds
1 tsp ground turmeric
1 tsp garam masala
Salt
Pepper
½ tsp sweet paprika
1 cup (190 g) split red lentils, rinsed
1 cup (240 ml) coconut milk
1⅔ cups (50 g) fresh spinach

To Serve

Juice of ½ lemon
Dried red chili flakes
Fresh cilantro, chopped
Plain vegan yogurt

BOK CHOY STIR-FRY

In the mood for some quick and delicious veggies? How about this street-style, stir-fried baby bok choy? It's the perfect leafy, nutritious side dish, bursting with garlic and a slight tanginess from the rice wine. This dish takes only minutes to make and has become a staple in our house.

Serves 2

Rinse and thoroughly dry the bok choy in a salad spinner. Place the oil in a wok or medium frying pan over medium-high heat. Add the garlic and ginger and stir-fry until they just begin to brown, 1 to 2 minutes. Add the rice wine and cook for 20 seconds, then add the bok choy and cook for 1 to 2 minutes, until it's beginning to wilt. Add the soy sauce, salt and pepper and cook, tossing with tongs, until the bok choy is tender, 2 to 3 minutes. Sprinkle with the sesame seeds to serve.

8 oz (225 g) baby bok choy, quartered

2 tbsp (30 ml) sesame oil

2 cloves garlic, minced

1 tsp minced fresh ginger

1 tbsp (15 ml) rice wine

1 tbsp (15 ml) soy sauce

Salt

Black pepper

½ tsp sesame seeds

MASSAMAN CURRY

As a dedicated peanut lover, massaman curry is everything I want in a good curry. It's a dish I order time and time again because I'm in love with the flavor profile: crispy fried tofu and lots of veggies, simmered in a peanutty spicy curry sauce inspired by Indian and Thai flavors.

Serves 4

To make the tofu, place the cornstarch, salt, turmeric and tofu in a small container, close with the lid and gently shake to coat the tofu cubes. Line a plate with some paper towels. Place the oil in a medium frying pan over medium-high heat and add the coated tofu. Fry on all sides until golden, then place on the lined plate and set aside.

To make the curry, place the coconut oil in a large pan over medium-high heat. Add the onion and sauté for 2 to 3 minutes, then add the garlic and ginger and sauté for another minute. Add the carrots, potatoes, massaman curry paste, red curry paste and sugar, and combine. Cook for 2 to 3 minutes, then add the coconut milk and 1 cup (240 ml) of water. Bring to a boil, then turn down the heat to a gentle simmer and cook for 10 to 15 minutes, until the potatoes are tender. Add the soy sauce, lime juice, peanut butter and some salt and pepper, and cook for another 2 to 3 minutes. Finally, add the fried tofu and combine.

Serve over cooked rice and top with cilantro, lime juice and chopped peanuts.

Fried Tofu

¼ cup (30 g) cornstarch

⅛ tsp salt

Dash of ground turmeric

14 oz (400 g) firm tofu, drained and diced

¼ cup (60 ml) neutral-flavor oil

Curry

2 tbsp (30 ml) melted coconut oil

1 medium white onion, diced

2 cloves garlic, minced

1 tbsp (7 g) minced fresh ginger

2 large carrots, diced small

4 medium russet potatoes, peeled and diced

3.5 oz (100 g) massaman curry paste

1 tsp Thai red curry paste

2 tsp (5 g) brown sugar

28 oz (830 ml) coconut milk

1 to 2 tbsp (15 to 30 ml) soy sauce

1 tbsp (15 ml) fresh lime juice

2 tbsp (32 g) peanut butter

Salt

Pepper

To Serve

2 cups (372 g) cooked basmati rice

Handful of fresh cilantro, chopped

Juice of ½ lime

¼ cup (35 g) chopped roasted peanuts

MANGO LASSI

This easy and refreshing vegan version of the lassi takes only minutes to make. It goes perfectly with Red Lentil Dhal (page 114) to balance the spiciness, or simply as a light afternoon drink. Make sure to use ripe mangoes for the best flavor. And if you are using frozen mango, leave out the ice.

Serves 2

Place all the ingredients in a high-speed blender and blend until smooth, 30 to 60 seconds. Pour into tall glasses and serve immediately.

1 cup (165 g) ripe fresh mango chunks, or frozen

1 cup (240 ml) plain soy or coconut yogurt

¼ cup (60 ml) coconut milk

1 to 2 tbsp (15 to 30 ml) maple syrup, or any liquid sweetener

¼ tsp ground cardamom

Handful of ice cubes

MATCHA ICE CREAM

Since my travels in Japan, I've been in love with matcha. This delicious green tea powder has tons of antioxidants and acclaimed health benefits. But most matcha ice cream served in restaurants is dairy-based, so I created my own version. It turned out rich and creamy and perfectly sweet. (You'll need an ice cream maker, but it's worth it!)

Serves 6

Place the cashews, together with all the remaining ingredients, in a high-speed blender and blend for 1 to 2 minutes, until smooth. Transfer the mixture to the fridge for 15 to 20 minutes to cool down.

In the meantime, prepare your ice cream maker as instructed. Pour the matcha mixture into the ice cream maker and turn it to the desired setting (I use "gelato," which is extra creamy) and let it run for 40 to 50 minutes, until the blade can't turn anymore. Transfer the ice cream to a freezer-safe container and either serve immediately for soft serve or freeze for another 1 to 2 hours for a firmer ice cream.

½ cup (75 g) cashews, soaked in water overnight, drained and rinsed

14 oz (420 ml) coconut milk

½ cup (120 ml) rice milk

½ cup (120 ml) maple syrup

1 to 2 tbsp (5 to 10 g) matcha powder

1 tbsp (15 ml) lime juice

Pinch of salt

COCONUT STICKY RICE

This popular Thai dessert brings back lovely memories of getting soaking wet during the rainy season and finding comfort in a plate of coconut sticky rice from a local street vendor. For me, it's the ultimate comforting dessert, with a fresh, tropical note thanks to the mango.

Serves 2 to 3

1 cup (200 g) glutinous sweet rice

1¾ cups (420 ml) coconut milk, divided

Dash of salt

⅛ cup (25 g) sugar

1 ripe mango, sliced

2 tbsp (18 g) toasted sesame seeds

Place the rice in a medium bowl and cover with water. Let it soak for 20 to 30 minutes, then drain. Add the drained rice with 1 cup (240 ml) of water and ½ cup (120 ml) of the coconut milk to a medium saucepan over medium heat. Add the salt and bring to a gentle boil. Lower the heat to a gentle simmer and close the lid. Cook for 17 to 23 minutes, until all the water has been absorbed. Take the pot off the heat. Let rest untouched for another 10 minutes.

In the meantime, add the remaining 1¼ cups (300 ml) of coconut milk and the sugar to a small saucepan and place over medium heat. Cook for 3 to 5 minutes, stirring continuously. Taste test for sweetness and add more sugar if desired. (It will be less sweet once it's added to the rice.)

When you're ready to serve, take a small bowl, pack it with rice and turn it upside down on a plate for a nice rice igloo. Pour some of the sweet coconut sauce on top, and circle with fresh mango slices and sesame seeds.

Organic
Avocado
250,- / kg
25,- / 100 g

LATIN AMERICA

Many foods that are common in Latin American cuisine, such as rice, beans and a variety of hearty fruits (such as avocado, plantains and jackfruit), are vegan, and many traditional dishes do not call for animal-based ingredients. That leaves a lot of room for creativity to celebrate the bright colors and flavors of Latin American cooking.

If you're a fan of creamy guacamole (page 132), loaded queso nachos (page 141), street-style elotes smothered in vegan mayonnaise (page 131) or the sweet taste of Brigadeiros (page 145), you'll want to sink your teeth into this chapter.

ELOTES

I have a fond memory of the street vendor on the corner of my Mexican high school supplying me with fresh elotes after school. While most street food elotes won't be vegan because they use dairy cheese and egg-based mayonnaise, I've created a delicious vegan version so we don't have to miss out on the fun. These are perfectly tender corn ears smothered in mayonnaise and covered in salty vegan cotija cheese. ¡Que rico!

Serves 4

Place a large pot of water over high heat. Add the salt and bring to a boil, then add the corn on the cob and cook for approximately 5 to 7 minutes. When the corn is cooked, remove it from the pot and let the ears cool down until they are safe to handle.

While the corn is cooling, prepare the cotija cheese. Place the almonds in a small food processor and pulse until you have fine crumbles. Add the remaining ingredients and pulse a few times more. Transfer to a bowl and set aside.

Prepare the spicy mayonnaise by combining all the ingredients in a narrow glass jar. Blend with an immersion blender until the mayonnaise is creamy. Add more milk to make it smoother or more oil to make it firmer.

When the corn is cool, put each ear on a skewer and rub it all over with lime juice. Brush each ear with spicy mayonnaise, then sprinkle the cotija cheese on top. Add some chili powder and cilantro to garnish.

Elotes

½ tsp salt
4 ears corn, shucked

Cotija Cheese

½ cup (75 g) blanched almonds
1 tsp lemon juice
½ tsp white vinegar
½ tsp garlic powder
¼ tsp salt

Spicy Mayonnaise

½ cup (120 ml) sunflower oil
¼ cup (60 ml) soy milk
1 tbsp (15 ml) lemon juice
Pinch of salt
1 tsp smoked paprika
½ tsp dried chili flakes

To Serve

2 tbsp (30 ml) lime juice
¼ tsp chili powder
2 tbsp (2 g) minced fresh cilantro

TOFU-WALNUT TACOS WITH GUACAMOLE

Tacos, with their various forms, fillings and shapes, hold a big space in my heart. During my exchange year in Mexico I basically lived off these hand-size filled tortillas. No matter the time of day, one or two tacos always goes well. Traditionally they are filled with different types of meat, but you can also find versions with beans, vegetables and cheese. My favorite version includes a deliciously crunchy tofu-walnut meat, lots of refried beans and a big dollop of guacamole on top.

Serves 2

To make the tofu-walnut "meat," place the tofu in a small bowl and use your hands or a fork to break it apart into small crumbles. Place the oil in a medium frying pan over medium-high heat. Add the tofu crumbles and sauté for 4 to 5 minutes, until golden, then add the onion and sauté for another 2 minutes. Add the garlic, walnuts, sweet and smoked paprika, chili powder, cumin, cayenne pepper and salt, and cook for 1 minute until fragrant. Finally, add the soy sauce and cook for another 1 to 2 minutes, until the tofu is nice and crispy. Remove the pan from the heat and set aside.

To make the refried beans, heat the oil in a medium saucepan over medium heat. Add the onion and sauté for 3 to 5 minutes, until translucent. Add the garlic, chili powder and cumin and cook, stirring frequently, until fragrant, about 40 seconds. Stir in the beans, together with ¼ cup (60 ml) of water, and combine. Stir, cover the pan, and cook for 4 to 5 minutes. Reduce the heat to low and mash up the beans with a potato masher or the back of a fork until they're mushy (you can leave some pieces or make it really smooth). Remove from the heat and add the lime juice, salt and pepper. Set aside.

To make the guacamole, place the avocados in a large bowl and mash them with a fork until smooth. Add the remaining ingredients and mix well.

(continued)

Tofu-Walnut "Meat"

7 oz (200 g) firm tofu, drained

2 to 3 tbsp (30 to 45 ml) neutral-flavor oil

½ large white onion, diced small

3 cloves garlic, minced

⅓ cup (40 g) finely chopped walnuts

1 tsp sweet paprika

½ tsp smoked paprika

¼ tsp chili powder

¼ tsp ground cumin

Dash of cayenne pepper

Dash of salt

1½ tbsp (22 ml) soy sauce

Refried Beans

1 tbsp (15 ml) extra-virgin olive oil

½ large white onion, diced small

2 cloves garlic, minced

¼ tsp chili powder

Dash of ground cumin

1 (15.5-oz (439-g)) can black beans, rinsed and drained

1 tsp lime juice

Salt

Pepper

Guacamole

2 ripe avocados, pitted and peeled

¼ red onion, diced small

5 cherry tomatoes, diced

¼ fresh jalapeño pepper, chopped (seeded for less spicy)

2 tbsp (2 g) chopped fresh cilantro

1 tbsp (15 ml) lime juice

Salt

Pepper

TOFU–WALNUT TACOS WITH GUACAMOLE (CONTINUED)

To serve, heat a large pan over medium heat. Place as many tortillas in the pan as will fit inside without much overlap. Add some tofu-walnut filling and refried beans and keep the tortillas on the heat for 30 to 40 seconds, until they're nice and warm. Transfer to a plate. Repeat with the remaining tortillas. Add some guacamole, onion and cilantro to each tortilla, and serve with lots of fresh lime wedges.

To Serve
10 tortillas
½ medium white onion, diced
Handful of fresh cilantro
1 lime, quartered

Note: If your tortillas have become a bit stiff, place them in a kitchen towel inside the microwave for a few seconds to soften them.

SWEET POTATO AND BEAN TAMALES

When I think of tamales I immediately remember the street vendor's high-pitched "Tamales!" shout as he moved through the neighborhood. Tamales are made of a filled corn dough that is steamed in corn husks or banana leaves. The fillings can vary a lot, but I love this hearty potato and black bean filling. Add some shredded vegan cheese to the filling, if you like. And don't forget to top your tamale with lots of pico de gallo, and maybe some slices of avocado.

Makes 12 tamales

Separate the corn husks and place them in a large bowl. Cover with hot water and let them soak for 30 to 60 minutes, until they're pliable. Drain and set aside.

To make the sweet potato and bean filling, place the oil in a medium skillet over medium-high heat. Add the onion and sauté for 3 to 4 minutes, then add the garlic and sauté for another minute. Add the tomato, jalapeño peppers, salt, pepper, chili powder and paprika and cook for 10 minutes. Add the cooked sweet potato and beans and cook for another 5 minutes. Using a potato masher or a fork, roughly mash the mixture to the consistency of refried beans.

To make the dough, place the masa harina, salt and turmeric in a large bowl and combine. Add the oil, sweet potato purée, broth and brine, and mix until well combined, adding more broth if needed (the dough should be spreadable).

To assemble the tamales, lay out a corn husk on a flat surface. Spread about 2 tablespoons (35 g) of the dough mixture on the top half, leaving some empty space along the sides. Add 1 to 2 tablespoons (62 to 32 g) of the filling in the center of the dough. Fold in the sides of the husk, then fold up the bottom. Use small strips of husk or simple kitchen string to tie the tamale shut. Repeat with the remaining ingredients.

(continued)

12 dried corn husks

Sweet Potato and Bean Filling

1 tbsp (15 ml) extra-virgin olive oil

1 small white onion, diced

2 cloves garlic, minced

1 small tomato, diced

1 tbsp (14 g) diced canned jalapeño peppers

Salt

Pepper

¼ tsp chili powder

½ tsp sweet paprika

¼ cup (35 g) diced sweet potato, boiled until soft

1 cup (172 g) canned black beans, drained and rinsed

Dough

2 cups (248 g) masa harina (see Note)

¼ tsp salt

Dash of ground turmeric

2 tbsp (30 ml) extra-virgin olive oil

2 tbsp (30 g) sweet potato purée

1 to 1½ cups (240 to 360 ml) vegetable broth, or more if needed

1 tbsp (15 ml) brine from canned jalapeño peppers

SWEET POTATO AND
BEAN TAMALES (CONTINUED)

Set a large pot of water to boil over high heat. Place the tamales, open side up, in a steamer basket and place that over the boiling water. Cover the basket, reduce the heat to a light simmer and steam the tamales for 50 to 60 minutes, making sure there is enough water in the pot at all times. Remove the tamales and let them cool down a bit before opening and serving.

While the tamales are steaming, make the pico de gallo. Place all the ingredients in a medium bowl and combine. Adjust the salt and pepper according to your taste. Let the tamales cool, then serve with the pico de gallo on the side.

note: Masa harina is not the same thing as cornmeal. It's actually dried corn dough, which is made from corn soaked in limewater. Many supermarkets carry it. You can buy dried corn husks for tamales at many grocery stores or online.

Pico de Gallo

½ large white onion, diced small

2 to 3 ripe tomatoes, diced small

3 tbsp (3 g) chopped fresh cilantro

¼ fresh jalapeño pepper, chopped (seeded for less spicy)

2 tbsp (30 ml) lemon juice

1 tbsp (15 ml) extra-virgin olive oil

Salt

Pepper

TAPIOCA CRÊPES

I discovered this tasty breakfast dish in 2016 during my travels in Brazil. These crêpes are a popular street food made with tapioca, a gluten-free starch that comes from manioc root (also known as cassava or yuca). You can add sweet or savory fillings, but I highly recommend a combination of vegan cheese and fresh veggies.

Serves 2

In a medium bowl, mix the tapioca starch, salt and pepper. Gradually add ¼ cup (60 ml) of water and the beet juice, stirring with a spoon as you go. The mixture should form small clumps that you can crumble with your fingers. You will know if you added too much water when the mixture will start to flow like a thick liquid (add more starch if that happens). Put the clumps in a sieve and press them through into a clean bowl.

Place a 7-inch (18-cm) nonstick skillet over medium heat and evenly sprinkle a thin layer of the starch mixture over the entire skillet (working fast here is a must). Even it out with the back of a spoon and cook for 30 to 40 seconds, until the crêpe is lightly golden brown. Flip the crêpe over and cook for another 30 to 40 seconds. Place it on a plate, add half the cheese, tomatoes and arugula to the crêpe. Season with salt and pepper and fold the crêpe over. Repeat with the remaining starch mixture.

Note: The crêpes should be served warm right out of the pan, as they stiffen quickly.

Crêpes

1 cup (122 g) tapioca starch
¼ tsp salt
Dash of pepper
3 tbsp (45 ml) beet juice

Filling

1 cup (112 g) shredded vegan mozzarella (page 22), or any mild vegan cheese
5 to 6 cherry tomatoes, cut in half
Handful of fresh arugula
Salt
Pepper

CHIPOTLE QUESO WITH NACHOS

While this is more of a Westernized dish, it oozes with great Latin American flavors, including cilantro, chipotle peppers and lime. This is the perfect starter to share with friends or family, and is 100 percent crave-worthy. As a bonus, you can store the queso in an airtight jar for up to three days in the fridge.

Serves 4

Place the potato and carrot in a small pot of water over high heat. Bring to a boil, then reduce the heat and simmer until soft, about 15 to 20 minutes. Drain, then place in a high-speed blender.

Add the butter to a small skillet and place over medium heat. Add the onion and sauté for 3 to 4 minutes, then add the garlic and sauté for another minute. Add the onion mixture to the blender together with the potato and carrot and blend briefly. Then add the cashews, rice milk, lime juice, adobo sauce, paprika, turmeric, garlic powder and ⅓ cup (80 ml) of vegetable broth and blend until smooth, 1 to 2 minutes. Add more broth if needed, until the queso is thick and creamy.

Transfer the queso to a serving bowl, and top with the cilantro, spring onion and tomatoes. Serve with the tortilla chips on the side.

Chipotle Queso

1 big russet potato, peeled and diced

1 small carrot, diced

1 tbsp (14 g) vegan butter

1 small yellow onion, diced

1 to 2 cloves garlic, minced

½ cup (75 g) cashews, soaked in water overnight and drained

½ cup (120 ml) rice milk

1 tbsp (15 ml) lime juice

1 to 3 tbsp (15 to 45 ml) adobo sauce, from canned chipotle peppers in adobo

1 tsp sweet paprika

¼ tsp ground turmeric

½ tsp garlic powder

⅓ to ½ cup (80 to 120 ml) vegetable broth

To Serve

1 tbsp (1 g) chopped fresh cilantro

1 spring onion, sliced

Handful of cherry tomatoes, quartered

1 (15-oz (425-g)) bag tortilla chips

AÇAI BOWL WITH NUTTY GRANOLA

Açai is the fruit of a palm tree that is native to South America. Açai bowls originated in Brazil. They are made of frozen açai that is puréed and served as a thick smoothie in a bowl or glass. They're typically topped with sliced fresh fruit, granola and honey. For the vegan version, try this deliciously crunchy homemade nutty granola and a drizzle of maple syrup. As a bonus, the granola will keep fresh in an airtight jar for 1 to 2 weeks.

Serves 2

Make the granola first. Preheat the oven to 350°F (175°C). Line a baking sheet with parchment paper.

In a large bowl, combine the oats, pecans, almonds, hemp seeds, flax seeds, flour, vanilla powder, cinnamon and salt. In a small bowl, combine the coconut oil and maple syrup. Pour the wet ingredients into the dry ingredients and stir until everything is fully coated. Spread the mixture evenly on the baking sheet and bake for 40 to 45 minutes, stirring halfway through. Remove from the oven and set aside to cool completely. Transfer to an airtight jar until you're ready to use it.

To make the açai bowl, break the bananas and açai purée into chunks and place them, together with the berries, in a high-speed blender. Add ½ cup (120 ml) of milk and blend on low speed. Scrape and press the mixture down and move it around to break everything up. Continue to blend until smooth, adding more milk only as needed.

To serve, divide the mixture between two bowls and top with some granola, strawberries, blueberries, banana slices and maple syrup.

Granola

1 cup (90 g) old-fashioned oats
⅓ cup (36 g) roughly chopped pecans
⅓ cup (36 g) chopped almonds
2 tbsp (20 g) hemp seeds
2 tbsp (14 g) flax seeds
2 tbsp (16 g) whole wheat flour
¼ tsp vanilla powder
¼ tsp cinnamon
Pinch of salt
⅓ cup (80 ml) melted coconut oil
3 tbsp (45 ml) maple syrup

Açai Bowl

3 medium frozen bananas, sliced
2 (3.5-oz (100-g)) packs frozen açai purée
1 cup (155 g) frozen blueberries
½ cup (75 g) frozen strawberries
½ to 1 cup (120 to 240 ml) almond milk

To Serve

Handful of sliced strawberries
Handful of blueberries
½ banana, sliced
Drizzle of maple syrup

BRIGADEIROS

Brigadeiros are small chocolate bombs—a traditional Brazilian dessert created by a confectioner from Rio de Janeiro named Heloisa Nabuco de Oliveira. The vegan version of these small, chocolaty delights is made with condensed coconut milk and high-quality dark chocolate for the ultimate rich treat.

Makes 12 to 15 balls

1 (14-oz (414-ml)) can full-fat coconut milk

2 tbsp (30 ml) maple syrup

1.5 oz (42 g) dark (70% cacao) vegan chocolate

Vegan chocolate sprinkles

Combine the coconut milk and maple syrup in a small saucepan and bring to a boil over medium heat. Lower the heat to low and cook for 1 to 1½ hours, until it's thick and reduced by half. It should not run off a spoon easily. Return the heat to medium and mix in the chocolate. Cook for 5 to 8 minutes, until the mixture is thick and creamy. Take the pan off the heat, pour the mixture into a small bowl and let it cool down. When it's at room temperature, place the bowl in the fridge for 2 to 4 hours.

When it has firmed up, scoop up about 1 tablespoon (15 g) of the mixture and roll it into a ball. Set the ball aside on a plate and repeat until you have used up all the mixture. Lay out the sprinkles in a plate and roll each ball in the chocolate sprinkles.

Acknowledgments

Writing a cookbook about two of my biggest passions is truly a dream come true. Integrating all those vivid foodie memories from my travels into a cookbook that shares little snippets of my journey with the world has long been a dream of mine, and I couldn't be more excited about this project. Publishing my second cookbook within two years has been a lot of hard work, but I wouldn't trade a minute of it. It has been an intense few months of recipe creation, taste testing and working until late at night. I'm so incredibly grateful for all the people supporting me in my life who helped with this project, by taste testing or mentally supporting me.

Chen, thank you for sharing my passion for delicious food and travel, as well as your constant love and support! You have brought so many new exciting flavors into my life and patiently endured these last few months as the number one taste tester.

Thank you to my amazing community of supporters and followers from around the world. Thank you for always trying my recipes, your sweet messages and inspiring me to continue sharing my recipes and travel adventures. You have made The Tasty K what it is today and I wouldn't be here without you! A special thank you to everyone who supported book number one and keeps on sharing delicious vegan holiday meals.

Gianna, thank you for being my rock. You have been there for me from the very beginning and you are quite possibly the coolest person I know. I can only hope to continue traveling the world with you as long as possible.

Thank you, Mom and Dad, for raising me to be the open-minded and curious person that I am. Thank you for giving me all the freedom I needed to find myself and explore the world at such a young age.

Finally, thank you so much to the entire team over at Page Street Publishing. Thank you for believing in me a second time and helping to turn my dream into reality. It has been a real pleasure working with all of you on my second cookbook, and I can only hope for many more to come!

About the Author

Kirsten Kaminski is the author, recipe developer and creative mind behind The Tasty K, a social media platform and recipe channel for vegan cooking and travel. As a self-taught photographer and videographer, she is trying to show the world how easy, healthy and delicious plant-based cooking can be. Her dynamic recipe and travel videos continue to go viral on social media with over 55 million views. Her work has been featured in *Thrive* magazine, Best of Vegan and feedfeed, and she has starred on German national television.

Despite growing up in a smaller city in Germany, Kirsten has always had a passion for traveling and has lived in nine countries over the past ten years. In 2019, she moved back to Germany and is currently exploring Berlin's vibrant vegan food scene.

If Kirsten is not in the kitchen trying out new recipes, you'll probably find her enjoying nature, working out or playing with her dog, Luna.

You can follow Kirsten's recipes and travels on Facebook (The Tasty K), or Instagram (@thetastyk). Check out her blog, www.thetastyk.com, for more information.

Index